P9-CDD-163

# THE FRAGILE UNIVERSE

# LIBRARY OF PHILOSOPHY AND RELIGION

*General Editor*: John Hick, H. G. Wood Professor of Theology,
University of Birmingham

This new series of books will explore contemporary religious understandings of man and the universe. The books will be contributions to various aspects of the continuing dialogues between religion and philosophy, between scepticism and faith, and between the different religions and ideologies. The authors will represent a correspondingly wide range of viewpoints. Some of the books in the series will be written for the general educated public and others for a more specialised philosophical or theological readership.

# The Fragile Universe

## An Essay in the Philosophy of Religions

Patrick Burke

**BOOKS**
10 East 53d St., New York 10022
(a division of Harper & Row Publishers, Inc.)

*First published 1979 by*
THE MACMILLAN PRESS LTD
*London and Basingstoke*
Published in the U.S.A. 1979 by
HARPER & ROW PUBLISHERS, INC.
BARNES & NOBLE IMPORT DIVISION

*Printed in Great Britain*

**Library of Congress Cataloging in Publication Data**

Burke, Thomas Patrick, 1934–
    The fragile universe.

    (Library of philosophy and religion series)
    1. Religion—Philosophy.  I.  Title.
BL51.B853        200'.1      78–17885
ISBN 0–06–490776–7

*Dorotheae matri*

# Contents

# Acknowledgements

Research cannot be carried on without financial support. At a time when such expenditures have come increasingly under fire, my colleagues at Temple University, faculty and administration, have given me generous support, enabling me to do field-work in Asia, the Middle East and the Mediterranean, and giving me time to write. Without them this book would not have been written.

I owe a personal debt of thanks to Michael Kerlin of La Salle College, and Eric Pyle of the University of Queensland. They gave liberally of their time and patience to scrutinise the entire essay, and helped substantially with the arrangement of the material.

My wife Marnie has been my best critic, and my most constant encouragement. Only the deepest gratitude can repay her unflagging interest, if it can.

# Introduction

The central topic of current philosophy of religion has been the meaning and the truth of the assertion that God exists. The roots of this preoccupation lie in the natural theology, and the criticism of that theology, of the eighteenth century in the West. The arguments of Hume and Kant are still the basis of contemporary discussion. While this attachment to eighteenth-century concerns may manifest a laudable sense of reverence for our ancestors, it has led the philosophy of religion into lamentable delinquencies and impoverishments.

One is that its notion of religion has been restricted in practice to Western theism, despite the advances of the last century in our knowledge of other kinds of theism, and of nontheistic forms of religion. A second is that attention is given exclusively to the rational or theological aspects of Western theism, while the dimension of lived or popular religion is ignored. But lived religion is part of the context of belief, and it is clearly a mistake to imagine that an idea, especially a religious idea, can be dealt with adequately if its context in life is ignored. A related defect is that religious conceptions are analysed from the aspect of their timeless logical properties, in abstraction from their historical dynamism or function. But one of the things we learned from the nineteenth century is that many properties and functions become associated with ideas only through the accidents of historical and cultural interaction, and cannot be evaluated appropriately if their historical and cultural context is omitted. Another defect regards method. The method of current philosophy of religion is conceptual clarification and analysis. It does not attempt the synthesis of common intuitions into a coherent understanding of the whole. Thus only one of philosophy's historically legitimate tasks, that of the criticism of arguments and general ideas, is undertaken, and the equally necessary enterprise of synthesis is neglected.[1]

What is now widely termed philosophy of religion is not a philosophising about the phenomenon of religion, which the name might be thought to mean, and long did, but a critique of 'natural' or philosophical theology. But contraries, as Aristotle observed, belong to the same genus. The criticism of philosophical theology is itself philosophical theology.

By contrast, the object of philosophy of religion as it is viewed here is to arrive at an overall picture of the phenomenon of religion, in more general terms and from a broader perspective than the particular sciences. That is, its aim is a theory of religion. To distinguish this sort of philosophy of religion, it has been termed here 'of religions'.

The main topics of a theory of religion are the nature and significance of the phenomenon of religion. I would like to make a case in this introduction that it is useful for philosophy and also for the study of religions that there be a coherent theory of religions, not only a psychological or a sociological one, but a philosophical one; and further, that since such a theory must be a work of synthesis as well as analysis, entailing roughness, approximations, inductive generalisations, and a groping with large obscurities, a legitimate role should be acknowledged for such a style of approach.

To give a preliminary illustration from the following text: religions are paths to salvation, broadly conceived; or perhaps more accurately, ways of living focused on salvation. This applies to truth-claims. Propositional truth is simply of no interest to religions except in so far as it is necessary for salvation. To imagine that any statement functions in religion primarily as an assertion of truth in a propositional sense will be to misunderstand it fundamentally. Not that its truth or falsity will be totally a matter of indifference. It is just that the point has been missed. It is as if someone were to tell a joke about the man in the moon, and a listener objected on the grounds that there really is no man in the moon.

The preceding paragraph suggests both the significance and the difficulties of the kind of approach advocated here.

It is useful for philosophy that there be a coherent and plausible theory of religions. The case for this is like the case for the philosophy of science, art, or history. Scientists may feel they obtain little benefit from the philosophy of science. Artists and historians may gain little from philosophies of art or history. But philosophy and philosophers benefit from these things. A theory of science, like a theory of history or art, presents us with a model that both integrates a diversity of shared perceptions about an important area into a consistent, structured picture of it, and enables us then to evaluate portions of it by their function in the whole, and the whole itself in relation to other significant areas. Aristotle's *Poetics*, Hegel's *Philosophy of History*, or Thomas

Kuhn's *The Structure of Scientific Revolutions* stimulate us to see ourselves and our own work in a new light, and provide a direction for our own thoughts. Aristotle's *Poetics* does one sort of job philosophy has been supposed to do: it gives us insight, of a general, abstract and fundamental order, into the nature and value of a prominent activity.

Similarly with religion. There is no reason to expect in advance that it will either profit or suffer from being theorised about. Some particular theories may tend to encourage or discourage religion or some forms of it, but the same is true of some theories about science and art. The aim of a theory of religion is neither to benefit nor harm religion, but to take an activity that has been extraordinarily prominent and at the same time profoundly puzzling and tantalising, and make sense out of it by pulling together dispersed intuitions into a structured, unified and coherent picture. Once we have a model of how the thing functions as a totality, we are in a position to assess it, to assess particular aspects of it by their place in the totality, and assign the totality itself its appropriate location in regard to other prominent fields.

This kind of thing was attempted by Whitehead, Santayana and Hegel among others. To the extent that their attempts are linked with methods or systems no longer popular, they have fallen into disuse. Since linguistic and conceptual analysis became the dominant mode in philosophy, no comparable attempt has yet been made. But what they were aiming at was essentially something desirable.

Another incentive may be added for having a theory of religion, from the standpoint of current philosophical theology itself. As we saw, this is a critique of natural

4

theology, and itself a form of natural theology. But theology, of whatever kind and including natural theology, must fall under the heading of religion. The animus that drives both theologian and anti-theologian is a religious concern. What is currently termed philosophy of religion then, it may be argued, is itself really a disguised species of religion, drawing on an inspiration at least akin to the religious. We need not look far in the literature, I think, for evidence that this is actually the case. The detachment appropriate to academic inquiry is not to be found in this form of religion more than in any other.

Not only is it advantageous for philosophy that there be a philosophical theory of religion, it is at least equally useful for the study of religions. Traditional Christian theology has fallen on harder times of late. In Europe it has suffered the thrusts of an existentialism that mocked attempts to make sense out of the absurdities of life. In the English-speaking world it has been mugged by logical positivists and language analysts. As a result many erstwhile or would-be theologians find themselves compelled to grapple with proofs for and against the existence of God, when they would really much rather be doing something else. Only there is nothing else for them to do: this is the nearest they can get to doing theology. They are happy to call it philosophy because that has a more scientific and academic ring to it, but they are not particularly interested in philosophy; by temperament and training they are not philosophers but theologians.

While traditional theology declines, the academic study of religions grows daily more robust. If we intend to have a department of religion, there are some basic fields we must cover: Christianity, Buddhism, etc., and of course 'philosophy of religion'. But who will teach philosophy of religion in a religion department, and what will he teach? The answer to the first question is: a frustrated theologian, not a philosopher, by and large—he will be found next door, in the philosophy department. What will the frustrated theologian teach? Why, theology, of course, that is, the nearest he can come to it in these regrettable days, i.e. natural theology, proofs and disproofs for the existence of the Judaeo-Christian God.

Now proving and disproving the existence of the Judaeo-Christian God contributes relatively little to the academic study of the general phenomenon of religion—no more than would attempts to prove or disprove the existence of the Tao or the Jainist *jiva*. It does not bring to light the laws by which religions operate, or their hidden structures. Much less does it help us evaluate the phenomenon of religion in general. It is an attack and a defense of one particular belief, a most important belief, but not one that exhausts the reality of religion. Of course if one side or the other could win a conclusive victory it would simplify the scene, but there is no immediate prospect of such an apocalyptic event.

By contrast, a philosophy of religion dealing with the nature and significance of religion at large can hardly avoid raising questions about the fundamental presuppositions that any student of any religion must employ. In doing this it can be a stimulus to other aspects of the study of religions, because it should relate to all of them, and thereby bring them into relationship with one another. The historian of Judaism and the lecturer in Zen Buddhism can cheerfully ignore each other in the interests of their own specialisations. It is not all that obvious at first sight that they can help one another much. But a general theory of religion, if it is coherent, must hold for both, and challenges each to take academic account of the existence of his neighbour. Are their fields really wholly unrelated, so that they have nothing whatever of interest to say to one another? Are they dealing with phenomena that are at bottom identical, and merely recounting the same story in different versions? What are their commonalities, and what are their differences?

Exploration of the nature and the significance of religion as such is presumably a philosophical inquiry. But the academic study of religion has so far attracted relatively few professional philosophers. It is significant regarding the state of the discipline that at the annual meeting of the American Academy of Religion, an immense body, the philosophy of religion has been thus far combined in one section with theology. The philosophical study of religion is not carried on in departments of philosophy; the resources for that are lacking there, namely familiarity with a broad spectrum of religions and religious phenomena. But it is also not carried on in departments of religion: these are typically populated by historians and theologians.

To build a theory of religion we require a method that emphasises synthesis rather than analysis. Common intuitions need to be brought into a consistent whole. Inductive generalisations, aiming at self-evidence, have priority here over analysis, argument, and proof. No doubt proof and conceptual clarification can never cease to be useful where they are available. But in comparison with the discernment of general patterns among widely dispersed events, the perception of hidden connections between things not apparently related, and intuitions of

7

totalities, their role is secondary, and an emphasis on them is misleading.

What I am proposing is thus open to attack by both religionists and philosophers. By philosophers because, at least at the beginning, and perhaps throughout, it must be content with inductive generalisations, imaginative synthesis, and appeals to general intuitions instead of a satisfying conceptual clarity and stringent argument; by religionists because it is neither theology nor history, but philosophy. The very lack of it, however, on these terms, may indicate to some a job to be done.

(These remarks are based mainly on observation of the present state of the discipline of philosophy of religion in the English-speaking world. However, as far as I can tell they have a general validity. In continental Europe, after a long period when the influence of existentialism and dialectical theology was paramount, the present trend in philosophy of religion, so far as there is one, is toward the kind of analysis being done in the Anglo-Saxon world. In the universities of India and the Far East the Anglo-Saxon model is also generally predominant.

(There are several individual exceptions to the situation I describe. Two especially stand out: the work of Ninian Smart and William Christian deserves to be clearly exempted from these castigations and remonstrances.)

Having advocated a programme, I should now probably indicate at least briefly how it might be carried out. How would one go about developing a philosophical theory of religion, and what would it look like? It seems there must be at least two main steps. The first is on the level of the empirical, and consists in looking at the data, that is, in acquiring familiarity with a broad range of the

8

things we put under the heading of religion, especially cross-culturally. An essential part of this, I believe, is direct exposure to other religions through personal experience of them in their cultural settings. It is idle to try to construct a theory of religion without stirring from one's armchair: it is necessary to look at religion, and see what is going on there. For this there is no substitute for travel. Lived religion cannot be discovered in books. Looking at the data means exposing oneself to as wide a variety of religious situations as possible. We do not know at first what will be important and what not.

The second step is an act of abstraction, and consists in allowing overall patterns to emerge from the data. This is a search for general structures and basic functions, not necessarily immediately obvious, but visible nonetheless, given careful scrutiny. This is analogous to seeing a figure hidden in a drawing: the riddle shows a picture of clouds and trees, but somewhere concealed in them there is a face. It is there to be seen, yet not everyone will see it, sometimes not even when it is pointed out to them. On the conceptual level such an operation, the perception of general patterns and structures, is an act of synthesis. It requires a unified intuition of a whole, comparable to seeing actions on the stage as a live drama, and not merely as isolated movements. No amount of analysis can be substituted for this, though all analysis presupposes it: we cannot dissect a thing into parts unless we have first seen it as a whole. However, just as analysis presupposes synthetic intuition, so really worthwhile synthesis comes only after analysis, after detailed scrutiny of the data, and the perception of differences, distinctions and dissimilarities. It is only when full justice has been done to the ways in which one thing is not another that we can say in

9

what ways they are the same. The affirmative judgement, as Hegel might say, requires first the labour and painfulness of the negative.

An important and difficult problem is the verification of such general patterns. They cannot be verified by empirical observation or conceptual analysis. How do you establish that there *is* a face among the clouds? The method of verification for such verdicts is more like that for legal or aesthetic judgements. If someone does not see that Jackson Pollock's *Cathedral*, or Henry Moore's *Reclining Figures* are fine art, you invite him to go back and look at them again, and then again, till he sees it. Perhaps he will never see it. Does that mean they are not good art?

But a voice may be raised in protest: What is the difference between the undertaking you have outlined and the well-known discipline of the phenomenology of religion? The phenomenologist of religion also proceeds inductively, acquiring familiarity with a broad range of religious manifestations and allowing overall patterns to emerge from them. He has long been preoccupied with the meaning of religious phenomena.

The patterns the philosopher seeks, however, are of a different kind from those of the phenomenologist. The phenomenology of religion is concerned with the meaning of particular phenomena within the religious system. What is the meaning of sacrifice? What is the significance of sky-gods, of rites of passage? It is the phenomenologist who notices that there are such things as rites of passage, to his great credit. But what the philosopher seeks is the nature and the significance of religion as such. What does it mean, to be religious? Where does religion fit into the scheme of human living? How does it relate to art and science, and to the variety of human cultures? What is its distinctive function? Is it a justifiable activity or is it without foundation, or are some forms of it justifiable and others not? The philosopher of religion asks about the meaning of religion in regard to life.

The pages that follow arise from dilemmas the author has encountered in trying to be religious reasonably. Thus their central concern is the tension between religion and reflection. The main aims of the essay are to clarify some aspects of this, and to see if possible what direction it leads in. These form the topics of the final two chapters. To pave the way for this it seems desirable to inquire into the nature of religion, and if possible to capture it for working purposes in a definition, which is attempted in the first chapter. But since empirical observation discloses most intimate relationships between particular religions and their particular cultures, we must ask to what extent such relationships hold of necessity and by the nature of the case. It appears that religions are necessarily culture-laden. This view is articulated, and some of its implications examined, in the second chapter. But while an investigation of the nature of religion and of its essential relationships is an inquiry into relatively timeless truths, no student of religion can fail to be struck by the astonishingly fortuitous character which the vicissitudes of human geography and history attach to even the highest conceptions of the spirit. Our noblest ideals prove to be in an important sense accidents of history, and we cannot overlook that in assessing them. The careers of some of the more prominent religious conceptions are described for this purpose in Chapter 3. Against this background the contemporary dilemma confronting anyone who attempts to be religious reasonably stands out, at least to my mind, acutely. Reflection threatens to alter the character of any religion radically. The nature of this threat is examined in Chapter 4, and some of the main alterations are described which reflection introduces inevitably and in general. But are there further alterations that reflection demands of religion with special force at this point in history? Is any particular direction indicated for the future career of religions? In the fifth chapter three principles fundamental to some religions are rejected as obsolete, and three others of a very general nature are suggested, which any future religion should take due account of, to do justice to the requirements of the present stage of our historical development. Thus the essay as a whole, taken with the author's earlier *The Reluctant Vision*, has in his mind the character and status of a prolegomenon to any future theology.

Like the former essay, this is an autobiographical document. Its title is no mere rhetorical device, but reflects a deep sense that the spiritual universes which alone infuse the highest meaning into our lives are yet accidental in the face of history, and frail and transient in the face of the questing human intellect.

# 1 Deliverance

The great religions are now everywhere in decline, as regards their hold on men's minds.[1] The claims of their doctrines have grown perceptibly less convincing. Multitudes whose loyalty yesterday was firm have deserted their allegiance. Calm certitudes that only recently resisted savage persecution have crumbled, and in many hearts where spiritual peace was once a reliable, if occasional, visitor, deep doubt and confusion have taken root. No doubt an intense enthusiasm is also apparent, and a determined clinging to traditions. But they are marked rather uniformly by a quality of shutting out the intellect, for fear.

What certitudes, if any, can take the place of the old? What banner can inspire a confidence comparable to the ancient? These decaying edifices of the spirit have been mighty.

Is this decay merely a painful passage to purer religion, or is it a wasting away of religion's very substance? Is it a decline of particular traditions, now become obsolete, and of merely traditional forms, or is it a withering away of religion itself?

To know where we stand spiritually in this time it would perhaps be helpful if we could attain to a clearer view of the nature of religion, and of religions. What does it really mean to be religious? Does it have any inner connections with traditions and institutions? Can there be such a thing as a secular religion? Can religion be identical with ethics? With psychology? If the realm of the transcendent is abandoned, is religion still religion? If we cease to hope for an ultimate deliverance?

To a certain extent the answers to these questions must lie in the future. What religion is will be revealed in what it becomes. But we can at least seek a greater clarity about our own ideas.

When I survey the many kinds of behaviour called religion, the one feature it appears to me they can safely be said to share is a focus on deliverance. What I have in mind is not ordinary deliverance, the ending merely of a particular dissatisfaction, but a cosmic deliverance, a deliverance with cosmic implications. A liberation is envisaged from what is significantly ill, which does not consist in mere annihilation, but is surpassingly great in its scope and importance. In the higher types of religion the significant ill and its remedy are spiritual or moral, but in folk religion they may be something as physical as drought and rain, or as small, from a broader perspective, as the loss and recovery of a familiar object. In any case the remedy for the ill is such that the nature of the universe is at stake in it. It seems to me that in every instance where we speak of religion, some reference is implied to such a cosmic deliverance, and that this reference is lacking in all the activities we hold not to be religious.

In the major religions, which have literatures and scriptures, the shapes of this deliverance have been delineated in detail, and often bear distinctive names. The religions of Indian origin focus on a deliverance from the ego or empirical self which is possible only in virtue of the ultimate nature of things: the *moksa* of Hinduism, the *nirvana* of Buddhism, and the related conception of the Jains, for which both terms are used; the religions of Chinese origin focus on a cosmic harmony, a union with heaven and earth; the religions of Semitic origin, Judaism, Christianity, Islam, on an ultimate reign of God. In the religions of non-literate peoples such distinct formulations are not so readily attainable, but the focus on deliverance of cosmic import is equally evident. The religions of the American Indians, for example, focus in general on an ultimate harmony with Nature surprisingly akin to that envisaged by the Chinese, and the religions of African origin on a well-being in this world to be bestowed by the powers that govern the universe. It would not be difficult to show that within the religious system everything has reference to the deliverance envisaged.

If we turn from particular traditions to features common to them, such as myths and rituals, the same focus on cosmic deliverance is evident. A religious myth will often provide an explanation of why things are as they are, but by that very fact, and at least as significantly, it points out a path to deliverance from the way things are. The words which the gods used to bring light out of darkness at the beginning will do the same now in our hearts; the cosmic egg from which the world was made exemplifies the present source of rebirth and fresh life.

In religious rituals the focus on cosmic deliverance is if anything even clearer than it is in myths. A rain dance, a sacrifice to obtain a blessing or to give thanks for one received, a divination to establish the quality of the time—all such ceremonies not only refer to some deliverance, but assume that the ultimate structure of things is at stake in it. A man performs a dance in order to obtain rain. What an immense harmony that assumes between such disparate things! It is not some particular technique devised for the purpose that is relied on (as when clouds are seeded with chemicals), but the very nature of the cosmos itself that is called into play.

It does not seem necessary to maintain that this cosmic deliverance is always the goal, or even the motive, at work in religion. But the notion of it is the main explanation of religious behaviour. If an unbelieving priest performs a ritual because the people think it efficacious, the motive of his action is the people's desire, not his own belief. But why do the people desire this particular ritual rather than, say, a military parade or a garden party? Because they believe that in some way this will be efficacious for a deliverance of cosmic significance, while those will not. The ceremony has its own nature, its own intention or purpose, a *finis operis*, apart from the purpose of the doer, the *finis operantis*. The community attributes to the action a species of intersubjective meaning independent of the individual carrying it out. For such reasons it seems preferable to speak of deliverance as the 'focus' of religion, rather than its motive or goal.

Although the term 'salvation' is often felt to have a specifically Christian flavour, it allows of being used in a much broader sense, and it would be convenient to use it so here, to stand for deliverance possessing cosmic implications.

The adjective 'religious' applies in ordinary language to anything whatever, including material objects, in so far as they belong to religion or a religion. A statue or a relic is a religious object. The noun 'religion', however, we invariably restrict to human *behaviour*. A relic is not religion, but the veneration of one is: a Quaker meeting house is not religion, but the silence observed in it is. Thus I can buy many things that are religious, but not religion, and an archaeologist may stumble on much that is religious, but he will never encounter religion. By behaviour I mean not only observable or external activity but purposive acts in general, including inner or unobservable ones.

If I may use these terms in these senses, then I believe religion can be defined as *behaviour focused on salvation*.

Deliverance is not necessarily to be conceived of as something in the future. In some traditions it is spoken of as already achieved or already present, only concealed and waiting to come to light. In this case it is the focus or main explanation of behaviour not as a goal to be attained, but as a reality to be manifested. Religion is then not a path to salvation, but a way of behaving that results from salvation. Religion can be either the cause or the effect of salvation. In either event salvation remains its object, its central consideration. Religion is activity arising out of the hope of salvation. Hope may refer to the future, but it can also refer to the present or the past. I can hope that the gentleman in front of me is telling the truth about the marvellous curative properties of the medicine he is selling, or that my Aunt Maggie really did think kindly enough of me to leave me that bequest in her will. Similarly I can hope not only that I will be saved, but also that I have been or am already saved.

The term salvation is perhaps liable to mislead, since it tends to suggest a deliverance which is absolute and total. However that is not the sense intended here. It would certainly be sufficient, but it is not necessary in order to have religion. By deliverance I mean deliverance from significant ill. While there are types of religion which envisage an ultimate deliverance from all ill, in many other instances of phenomena which we style religion, the deliverance looked to, although of such a nature that it has cosmic implications, is nevertheless in itself modest. Thus a life spent trying to do God's will, and hoping for his blessing in some general sense without expectation of a future life; or a striving to attain humanity of heart, compassion and wisdom, not for some future recompense but for their own sake as ultimate and transcendent values (as may be found in the Confucian tradition) deserve to be accounted religion at least as much as a sacrifice offered for rain, or a prayer for a safe journey: it is the cosmic significance of the deliverance, not the elimination of all ill, that is decisive.

Special problems seem to be raised for the definition I have offered by some cases. If deliverance from ill is indeed envisaged, but for the future members of some group ethnic or economic, i.e. the group as group, such as the Jewish people, the proletariat, or the human race, rather than for individuals, does this qualify as salvation? There has been much we would want to call religion where the deliverance of the tribe or nation is a most prominent concern. But in all the cases where we customarily use the term religion, however prominently the fate of the group may figure, the fate of the individual is also always important. Public religion in Athens and Rome was for the cities of Athens and Rome, but also for the individuals who made the offerings to the gods. If the deliverance of the individual is entirely ruled out as a matter of conern, I believe there is no case where we incline to speak of religion. Salvation is eventually in some sense always of the individual. Presumably this is one reason why there is a general reluctance to apply the term 'religion' in a strict sense to communist and fascist movements that in other respects have a strong resemblance to religions.

It might seem that there is an important form of religion to which the conception we have suggested, and especially the notion of deliverance, does not apply, namely mysticism. For the mystic sees and seeks the oneness of things, and thus in some sense finds everything acceptable. He affirms rather than negates, embraces rather than rejects. He does not base himself on any problematic dimension of life. His desire is not to save himself, but to lose himself, in an ultimate union, whether of knowledge or of love. But in saying this, we have already pointed to a form of deliverance as his goal, namely, that he seeks to be saved from himself, from the finitude of his own existence and the particularity of his own ego. Not from his real or ultimate self, necessarily, but from his ordinary or empirical self he either desires deliverance or sees it as in some sense already true.

It may seem that the account we have given of religion makes it more self-centred than it often is. Deliverance as we have described it is something that happens at the least, and even mainly, to the individual. But there are forms of religion, and those with some claim to be the nobler and more spiritual, that positively discourage concern for one's own salvation. If a person loves God for the sake of loving God, without thought for his own fate, is that not religion? The Buddhist may tell the Christian: Your desire for a continued personal existence in heaven is a gross egocentricity, and the first thing you must be rid of, if you are to make spiritual progress.

But salvation, though it is of the self, is not necessarily something selfish. During the European Middle Ages there was disagreement between Duns Scotus and Thomas Aquinas about the essence of heaven. Aquinas held it to consist in the vision of God, Scotus in the love of God. For the one it was bliss (though a bliss one had to be worthy of), for the other it was spiritual perfection (though a perfection that entailed supreme joy). A comparable disagreement separates the Theravada from the Mahayana Buddhist. The former has as his aim the straightforward and steadfast pursuit of deliverance. The latter sees his ideal in the one who refuses deliverance for the sake of helping others to reach it, though by that very fact he attains spiritual perfection, and so deliverance. In many forms of religion spiritual perfection, which is entirely unselfish, has a status superior to any ultimate happiness, and by itself constitutes salvation.

Of course it is possible to pursue unselfishness in a selfish way: I would be more perfect if I were unselfish, therefore I will endeavour to be unselfish. Most religions, as a matter of common sense, discourage this. But it is not easily avoided. If a person has once reached the point where his quest for spiritual perfection is thoroughly unselfish, then by that fact he is already spiritually perfect, and on at least one account has attained deliverance.

Any activity focused on salvation presents us with an instance of religion. But 'a religion' is something further. The term suggests not isolated instances of behaviour, nor isolated religious objects, but a sweeping programme and a settled way of living. It may be simple in its outline, but it is an entire system.

We speak of 'a religion' in regard to both institutions and individuals, with interesting differences. More commonly we mean by 'a religion' a historical movement, a form of social organisation. Islam is a religion, and so is the religion of the Ashanti. Taken in this sense of a public institution, a religion embraces a devastating ambiguity between the ideal and the lapse from the ideal. When we speak of Christianity, we may have in mind a particular set of high ideals that emerge in history in the wake of Jesus of Nazareth. In this sense it is a mark of Christianity to love your neighbour. But equally we may mean by Christianity the historical career of these ideals in the world, the institution we call the Christian Church. In this sense it is also a mark of Christianity to have been intent on power and hypocritical, to have sponsored inquisitions and witch-hunts, in short, to fear and hate one's neighbour. Some would like to call one of these 'true' Christianity and the other 'false'. But each is as real as the other, and any definition we give of 'a religion' must make room for the abyss between them.

Sometimes by 'a religion' we have in mind the religion of an individual. Increasingly people speak of 'my religion': 'my religion is myself'. By this a person frequently means, I must have something to believe in, something to base my life on. I find nothing I can believe in but myself. I have confidence in myself and my own abilities, and my main aim in life is to be true to myself and to develop my potentialities to their fullest. Thus 'my religion' expresses an intention, a supreme value, an ideal. It has no room for lapses, deficiencies and fallings away. It is unburdened by the ambiguity of institutions. In the third person it may be used disparagingly: 'his religion is making money'. But even this maintains the sense of devotion to something held in the highest esteem. If in a moment of weakness he makes a donation to charity, we do not ascribe this to his religion of making money, as we ascribe inquisitions, crusades, and hypocrisy to Christianity.

A question this chapter opened with was, can there be religion without religions? Clearly this question applies only to institutional religions, not to personal ones. The occurrence of any instance of religion, even, say, a pilgrimage organised for profit, presupposes at least some personal religions. The question arises at all only because there are people who are religious and desirous of having a religion, but who feel unable to associate themselves with any available institutional religion. What are they to do? What the question asks is whether personal religion is likely to survive or maintain any substance without the support of institutional religion. An answer to the question will depend on what we understand by 'a religion'.

What is a religion? How can we tell one when we see one? Is the religion of a solitary individual really 'a religion?' The train of thought followed thus far suggests that a religion is *a way of life focused on salvation*, in the sense explained.

This definition has the virtue that it allows for both the individual and the institution. But what is a way of life? It might seem that this notion is too vague and loose to be useful. However, in the context of cultural anthropology its usefulness has already been demonstrated.[2] A way of life can be viewed as having at least two levels, an explicit or surface structure and an implicit or depth structure, a distinction familiar in other areas. The surface structure of a way of life consists in the observable regularities of the behaviour of an individual or a group. Its depth structure consists in the underlying, that is, unobservable interest patterns that maintain and explain the surface structure.[3] We shall have occasion to return more fully to these later.

To have a way of life focused on salvation, then, means on the one hand to have regular patterns of observable behaviour possessing as their main specific explanation salvation, or a deliverance possessing cosmic implications. Festivals, the practice of patience, collections in church and a habit of meditation might be examples, without question of motive. On the other hand it also means having patterns of interest centring on a cosmic deliverance. Here motive is supreme. In the case of an institution, such as Islam or Judaism, at least some persons must be motivated by salvation, enough to support the visible structure, if the institution is to be a religion. In the case of a single individual, he will have a religion and be entitled to speak of 'his religion' to the extent that some form of cosmic deliverance is a prominent and effective motive in his way of life. But if what he really means is just that his central concern in life is to be true to himself and develop his own potential, and that this preoccupation is a substitute for expectations of a cosmic deliverance, then his claim to have a religion is extravagant.

The question of the nature of religion can be posed in one form as a question about its very existence. Is there really such a thing as 'religion' in the general sense of the term? The notion is applied to such a diversity of things that they appear to have nothing significant in common: it does not seem there is any one single thing that 'religion' stands for. The term is employed for some of the lowest and most degraded practices, yet it is also used of the loftiest attainments of the human spirit; it is applied equally to human sacrifice and to selfless love for one's neighbour, to absurd superstitions as well as to profound wisdom, it is used for inner piety unconnected with any external rituals, and of external rituals empty of any piety, of noble ideals and of institutions that never live up to them. Arguably, the notion has been stretched so wide that it has no significant content left. Thus John Dewey finds the difference among religions 'so great and so shocking that any common element that can be extracted is meaningless.'[4]

A further consideration is that the notion of religion is a Western one only, occurring in languages that have derived it from the Latin, and in Arabic, and in very few others. There is no equivalent for it in classical Chinese, Japanese or Sanskrit, for example. That is, most cultures do not distinguish what we call religion from other aspects of life: the things we separate out and assign to the sphere of religion they view as an integral part of life. The notion that there exists a distinct realm of religion implies that there also exists a realm of the nonreligious or secular. To impose such a distinction on cultures that do not recognise it appears to be artificial and misleading.[5] The distinction between the religious and the secular has received a special emphasis in the religions of Semitic origin, with their idea of a God who creates a world distinct from himself and therefore in some sense possessing an independent existence. The use of the term 'religion' for them therefore may well be appropriate, but its extension in a general sense to other cultures may be questioned.

The conclusion of these arguments is that there is really

no such thing as religion, in the singular, general sense; or, what is the same thing, that the notion is not very useful; at most there are religions, in the plural.

However, the existence of religions in this sense may also be questioned. Candidates for the position of '*a* religion' are usually such things as Christianity or Islam. These are historical movements, most have long histories behind them, and even the most recent has passed through many vicissitudes. They have undergone bewildering changes. What shall we count as Buddhism? The teaching of the Buddha, eschewing both popular religion and metaphysics, or the movement that subsequently grew up after him in India, reinstating both popular religion and metaphysics with zest, or the quest for the Pure Land? What shall we count as Christianity? The thoroughly Jewish teaching of Jesus, the Hellenistic mystery saviour religion of Paul, the Roman organisation and detailed ritual of Catholicism, the silence and moral rectitude of the Quakers? Where is the continuity, where is the unity, that would entitle us to put all these historical diversities under one name? How can we view any historical movement as '*a* religion'?

Let us take the last of these difficulties first. It turns on the discontinuity of history. History implies change, what comes after is not the same as what went before. The logical conclusion of the argument is that no historical movement maintains an identity. This must apply not only to religions but to anything whatever that exists in history. No historical entity can be continuous. But such an argument proves too much. For change to take place, there must be something that stays the same, otherwise you do not have change at all, but the disappearance of one thing and its replacement by another. The transient implies the abiding. Discontinuity presupposes continuity. History contains both, and it is the job of a good historian to do justice to both. The identity of a historical movement is the unity of a causal chain of events, and is lost when that particular stream of causality dries up. Whether a particular historical movement changes so radically that it must be said to have suffered that fate is a question to be pursued from case to case. It cannot be asserted as a general principle that historical movements lack identity. On those grounds we could never be entitled to speak of 'a historical movement' at all. It may be that some of the things we call religions have changed thus drastically. But that does not rule out the existence of religions.

From another angle the argument defeats itself. To claim that what we consider religions are historically too discontinuous to be bundled together under the same labels, to assert that later Christianity is a different movement from earlier Christianity, or later Judaism from earlier Judaism, is to imply not that there are no religions, but that there have been more of them than we thought.

As for the argument that in many societies what we call religion is not a distinct facet of life but an integral and indistinguishable part of the whole, has no name, and constitutes no recognised category, this is a valuable observation about the nature of some cultures, but says nothing about the reality of religion or the usefulness of the idea of it. No social science could endure for an instant that was impressed by such an argument. It may well be that many inhabitants of New Guinea have no special word for politics or philosophy, but it would be fallacious to conclude on that account that they do not practice politics and do not philosophise, that the idea of politics in their case is artificial and misleading. It merely means we have an idea, a category, a way of unifying our perceptions of things that they have not. We may be sure they have ideas we have not. The value of an idea must be judged on other grounds than whether it is itself utilised by the people it is applied to. In particular the value of the idea of religion will depend on whether we can find something fairly clear that it refers to.

As regards the argument that there is no such thing as religion in the general sense of the term, because of the great diversity among the objects it is extended to: the mere fact that a notion is applied to a wide variety of things is scarcely cause for astonishment. All it requires is the modest minimum that they have sufficient in common. Behind this difficulty lies typically a confusion between two senses of the word religion, one descriptive, the other evaluative. For many people the notion of religion represents primarily an ideal, having to do with whatever is of ultimate significance, of the utmost importance, or supremely to be valued, so that it can be said everyone *ought* to be religious. This view finds expression in such definitions as 'ultimate concern', or 'ethics tinged with emotion'. Where religion is viewed solely as an ideal, sometimes called 'true religion', then of course it cannot include superstition, human sacrifice or hollow ceremonial. It is significant that Dewey, who has pressed this objection most forcefully, finds the differences between religions not merely an intellectual difficulty, but a reason for moral outrage: he is shocked at them.[6]

From this view the common use of the term religion in a purely descriptive sense, to denote a certain set of historical facts irrespective of their merit, is unjustifiable. The fact of religion, as we experience it in established institutions and the private lives of individuals, contains much that is very far from ideal. In one sense religion can stand for an ideal; in another sense it may stand for the very opposite of the ideal. What can these two possibly have in common, the ideal and the fact that contradicts it? What justification can we have for putting them together under the same roof, dignifying the sordid facts of history with the mantle of high ends, and besmirching noble dreams with the squalor of reality?

This problem is part of the larger ambiguity of being human. It is given to human beings alone that they can either be or not be 'human'. What does it mean, to be 'human'? It is inhuman to be cruel: it is also rather typically human. Man is the only being who by his very nature has the power to fall away from his own nature. A bird cannot be unbirdlike: an amoeba cannot be anything other than amoebalike. They are always simply true to their nature. With us it is different: we are born human, yet the achievement of humanity is a lifelong task. In one sense being human refers to a fact: the way people actually are. In another sense being human is a moral ideal: the way people ought to be.

Yet it is not as if there were no bond between these two. It is part of the way people actually are that they can entertain moral ideals, and that moral ideals apply to them whether they entertain them or not. Moral ideals are real: people have them, and they are bound by them even if they do not have them. Thus we are justified in saying that being human means both the ideal and the fact that contradicts the ideal. Living up to the ideal of being human is marvellously and truly human. And falling away from the ideal of being human is regrettably, but no less typically, human.

Just as there is humanity and there is inhumanity, and inhumanity is human yet not human, so there is true religion and false religion, and false religion is truly religion yet not religion. This ambiguity touches everything that belongs to our race. It does not mean there is no such thing as religion, any more than it means there is no such thing as humanity, or that the respective concepts are useless.

We may proceed, then, with some assurance that religion exists, and even some religions. By itself however this tells us little about what religion really is, what *a* religion is, or what the difference between them. Religion exists now. But will it continue to exist? If religions are in decay, is not religion? If existing religions disappear, what will take their place, if anything?

Partly this is a matter of predicting the future, something better left to economists, groundhogs and other experts. But it is also a matter of *recognising* the future. Would we be able to tell religion in the future if we saw it? Would we be able to tell Christianity or Judaism in the future if we saw them? It is sometimes difficult enough to tell them now. Even the most religious people often do not know with any precision what is religion and what is not. Thus recognising religion in the future is not likely to be anything different from recognising it now. It is a matter of understanding the nature of religion, despite its guises.

What sort of behaviour qualifies for the designation 'religion'? What are the minimal conditions for the use of the term? They must be fairly wide, as we have seen, wide enough to encompass such contrasts as adherence to ideals and the falling away from them, empty ritual and sincere sacrifice, which seem to have little in common. Typically definitions of religion have been unable to embrace this diversity. Thus the idea of 'ultimate concern' may well apply to the more interior forms of religion, but it does not include purely exterior manifestations. The unbelieving priest's offering of a sacrifice to the gods because the people wish it will be counted as religion by any anthropologist, but is scarcely a case of ultimate concern.

Something similar holds for the notions of the holy, and the sacred. Certainly they have been of the utmost importance in the history of religions. But they are usually associated with personal conceptions of divinity, and typically are lacking where these are lacking, notably in some forms of Buddhism, especially Zen, and Confucianism, which are nevertheless accounted religion. The related notion of the numinous is suggestive, but vague.

Promising attempts have been made to establish the common element in religion in terms of transcendence. But so far, despite much attention, this has not proved a very satisfactory notion to work with. If the transcendent is understood as an entity, there are religious traditions that reject such a conception. If it is understood as a state, a state is always a state of someone, and there are traditions that reject the notion of individual personhood necessary for such a state. If it is understood as an event, the act of self-transcendence, it does not appear that this applies to the simpler and more exterior forms of religion. If it is described solely in negative terms, it is not clear on what grounds it is then called transcendent, which seems to imply something positive.

Attempts to define religion sometimes meet with strong reservations. Some feel that religion is such a rich and varied thing it is a pity to circumscribe it within the conceptual limits of a definition. To imprison the dramatic and elemental force of religion within the cage of a definition is to wring the life out of it, and leave it arid and sterile, it is felt. But it is surely a legitimate task for the philosopher of religion to try to understand the nature of religion, and that is what a definition tries to capture, at least for working purposes, in useful brevity. It would be a mistake to use a definition as a device to cut off discussion, or discourage open-minded investigation of the diversity of phenomena, on an assumption that 'now we know what religion is' and we do not need to look any further. A good definition provides us with working guidelines to enable us to distinguish between different classes of things, and to recognise members of a class when we encounter them.

Again, the claim we have already examined that there is no such thing as religion, because the wide variety of things called religion appear to have no single element in common, is also made in the form of a claim that religion cannot be defined. The use of the term is then often said to be based on 'family resemblances'. But 'family resemblances' is not an ultimately satisfactory explanatory concept. It leaves an unexplained diversity. It is doubtful whether the notion is even coherent, in the technical sense usually given it since Wittgenstein. AB and CD are supposed to resemble one another, or at least to belong to the same group, because AB resembles BC, having the feature B in common, and BC resembles CD, having the feature C in common. But in that case AB and CD will not resemble one another, because they have no apparent feature in common, and the only grounds for putting them together in the same group can be that we know from other sources that they do have a feature in common, such as blood relationship. Thus an appeal to family resemblances in this sense is no substitute for an attempt to discover the nature of the things in question, and is rather a sign of intellectual bankruptcy. If there is no common feature among the members of a group, there is no reason for designating them a group. That they are in fact widely held to be a group is therefore either a mistake, or else it is left unexplained.

In passing it may be remarked that Wittgenstein, who elaborates this notion of family resemblances in developing his idea of language-games, is not interested in explanations, and makes no serious attempts to discover whether the things called games actually have common elements or not. Despite his injunction to 'look and see', he assumes they do not, in the interests of his utilitarian theory of meaning, and selects his examples to fit this preconceived notion (*Philosophical Investigations*, para. 65ff.). But suppose I look and see, and find they do have common elements? For a large number of occasions, though not necessarily all, on which we use the word game, at least the definition given by the Oxford English Dictionary seems to fit quite neatly: 'an amusement or diversion in the form of a contest' (And whoever thought that amusements had to be *amusing*, as Wittgenstein's *unterhaltend* is translated? *ibid.*, para. 66).

This is not, of course, to reject what I take to be the ordinary notion of family resemblance, namely that the members of some families often have one or more distinctive features in common. This will be utilised somewhat in the next chapter. Nor is it to be generally unsympathetic to Wittgenstein's praiseworthy insistence that we keep in mind the way words actually function in live situations, and do not allow ourselves to be bewitched by their sometimes misleading appearances.

There is no difference between defining a thing and defining the notion of the thing: to define the notion of a table is to define a table. This is not the same thing as a report on linguistic usage. If I want to know what a square root is, you may inform me that sometimes the term might be used to indicate vegetable roots that are square rather than round or oblong, but mostly it is used as a term for that component of a number which, when multiplied by itself, produces the number. By telling me how the word is used you have also, it is true, pointed to the nature of the things it stands for; but what you have primarily been doing is informing me of a custom people have in speech, not explaining the nature of a mathematical entity, except incidentally. A report on linguistic usage can always be verified in principle by experiment; for example, we could take a survey of the way people use the term, and that would confirm or deny the report. But this is by no means always the case with a definition. A report on the way a word is used is preliminary to definition. If we find it is used of different things, we are still left with the question, what is the nature of any one of these things?

Also, a definition is not to be confused with a stipulation of linguistic usage, as when someone says: For the purposes of this discussion, I mean by the term man any member of the human race, regardless of sex. He is indicating how he wishes his language to be understood, not explaining the nature of man.

What grounds does the definition I have given rest on?

While the definition of purely formal concepts, such as a square root, may be dependent on an examination of linguistic usage, and is likely to be arrived at by analysis of the notion itself, by contrast the definition of an empirical fact, such as religion, cannot be arrived at in this way, but must be an inductive generalisation. That is, it must rest on a scrutiny of the phenomena generally acknowledged to be instances of religion, and on a search for their common features. An inductive definition cannot be proved, but only disproved. The definition of religion offered here would be invalid if an instance could be given which is generally acknowledged as religion, but which the definition fails to cover, or if the definition includes something not generally considered an instance of religion. If I adduce this particular definition of religion, it is because I believe there are no counter-instances to it, and because it appears to me there are counter-instances to the other definitions that have been suggested. Thus in proposing a definition I am appealing to the reader's breadth of acquaintance with the variety of things designated 'religion', and to his intuitions regarding their common features. If I am asked what grounds the definition rests on, I can only reply that it has been suggested by my own study and experience of religious phenomena, and that I can discover no case of anything recognised as religion where it does not hold, and nothing else where it does.

Can there be such a thing as secular religion? If the secular is taken as the opposite of the religious, then clearly not. More properly the secular contrasts with the sacred. In the major or higher religions, with which we are especially concerned here, feelings of sacredness are typically associated with personalised conceptions of divinity, as noted earlier. 'You shall be holy, because I, the Lord your God, am holy'. A personal God is supremely attractive, and also dreadful. He rewards those who honour him, and punishes those who transgress his laws. Sacred is that which belongs to him, and it is set sharply apart from the lesser affairs of men because it is his, who is to be loved above all, and also to be feared above all.

In the idea of salvation as such there is nothing that requires the concept of a personal God, and so nothing that requires the notion of the sacred. As long as a deliverance of cosmic import from significant ill is envisioned, the requirements for salvation are met. There are some conceptions of salvation that rest on the idea of a personal God, notably in the religions of Semitic origin, and those religions cannot retain their traditional identity in a secular form. There are other conceptions of salvation that do not rest on any idea of a personal God, notably in some forms of Buddhism, and in the Confucian tradition, and such religions are naturally secular.

Can religion be identical with ethics? Ethical values are often thought to have a clear nobility and dignity over other values. A person forced to choose between doing serious moral evil on the one hand and personal survival on the other not only can but should choose to die well than to live ill. The identification of religion with ethics has been forcefully defended, and widely spread, by liberal Protestant Christianity, which itself, so far as the content of its belief goes, may be considered identical with ethics. The question resolves itself into the question, whether ethics, simply of itself and without further addition, can be considered a way of life focused on salvation. The answer seems to be, it is not necessarily, but it may be. It is not necessarily: in the West we have traditions of ethical religions (Judaism, Christianity, Islam) which hold out promise of a deliverance from all ill, in union with God, on condition of an ethical life. The reason for the condition is that God himself is supremely ethical, and only an ethical life renders one worthy of union with him. (There is also a version of Christianity according to which an ethical life is the only fitting response to God for a deliverance already granted.) The connection between the ethical life and salvation is more than extrinsic, but the salvation envisaged does not lie in the ethical life itself, but in God. In the ethical religions of the West ethics has traditionally been directed towards a salvation distinct from it, in virtue of a divine revelation. In these cases ethics alone by itself cannot be considered to make out the whole of the religion, and religion is not identical with ethics simply of itself and without addition.

In the West we also have a tradition of nonreligious ethical philosophy, stretching from, say, Aristotle's *Nicomachean Ethics* to modern philosophical ethical theory and action, which entertains no notion of salvation.

On the other hand it is possible to approach the ethical life from the standpoint that it itself constitutes an adequate deliverance from at least significant ill. This is exemplified in some strands of the Confucian tradition. In this case something that we might call ethics itself equals salvation, constitutes a deliverance of cosmic import, and religion is then identical with ethics.

A similar question is, can religion be identical with psychology? The aim of psychology, so far as concerns us here, is mental and emotional well-being. If a person lives his life in such a way as to maximise his mental and emotional well-being, does this not correspond to our description of a religion? As psychology is currently practised professionally, its aim is not so much to eliminate psychological distress, as to enable a person to reach a satisfactory level of emotional adjustment to the world he lives in. The starting point of psychology is not ordinary everyday life as such, but pathological states which render the individual unable to cope with ordinary strains and stresses. In its professional, Western form it does not point to a cosmic deliverance.

It is possible, however, to regard ordinary, everyday life as we commonly experience it, with its emotional vicissitudes, its ups and downs, its tensions and releases, its attractions and repulsions, as itself a pathological state. In this case it is not some particular aspect of life, but life itself, existence itself as we know it, that is the problem to be solved, the disease to be healed. A programme for such healing does indeed point to a cosmic deliverance, and will qualify as religion: it can be said to constitute a way of life focused on salvation. This description applies in general to the major religions of Indian origin, Buddhism, Jainism and Hinduism, especially in their more reflective or philosophical rather than popular, devotional forms. Of early Buddhism above all it may be said that it is psychology transformed into religion. Just as, in the case of Judaism, Christianity and Islam, we may say with some justification that they are ethics transformed into religion.

A religion is a way of life focused on salvation. But the religions we have inherited are quite special and particular ways of life, animated by special and particular conceptions of salvation. The circumstances of their origin are now remote, their voices have become alien, they carry the burdens of centuries, jewels and tinsel,

37

treasures and trivialities, clasped preciously in their arms without distinction. What deliverance can they now offer us, these venerable but tottering invalids of the spirit?

To be in a better position to answer this question, it may prove useful first to investigate the nature of their identity.

# 2 Culture

The traveller through the regions of the Nile and the Ganges, if he passes by the stagnant ponds the currents have dug out and abandoned, will see lotuses rising out of the slime and ascending through the muddy water, leaving the surface behind and climbing up into the air, and opening their buds, bursts of colour spurning the touch of the water and dirt that bears them. If such a flower grew only in the beautiful places appropriate to it, it might leave the observer unmoved. But its detachment from its squalid home is striking. It seems a natural symbol of purity, of wisdom, of the yearning to leave behind the sordid and low, to be untouched and virginal, to ascend to the exalted realm of the ideal and the spirit. Thus the lofty dreams that stir our hearts gather shape and energy from the very slime they reject. The ideal beyond history emerges out of the mud of history, in the shifting tides of act and passion that pit men against each other and themselves, isolate them from one another, and draw them briefly together.

A dream of the eternal lies on my soul, a longing to be freed from the tyranny of transience. But my soul has its very roots in the transient, it inhabits a place and a time, and the shapes of its dream, too, have homes, have their own places and their own times. The eternal has a history and a geography. Its shades and shadows have taken form slowly, over eras and epochs, they have migrated across borders and seas and distances, from people to people. I have inherited my dreams. Only in forms does the Formless come to us, and though they appear to be obvious and necessary, they are accidents. The manifestations of the Eternal are temporary, the embodiments of the Absolute are relative, the incarnations of the Necessary are matters of chance.

*      *      *

If we consider the major religions in regard to their most prominent differences and similarities, they form three families: those of Indian origin, those of Chinese origin, and those of Semitic origin. The religions of African origin constitute a family, and those of the American Indians another. Within each of these groups the similarities are more striking than the differences; between the groups it is the differences that stand out. This holds true whether we look at the symbols they make use of, or their world-views.

This fact is remarkable. The principle by which religions resemble and differ from one another is not religious, but cultural. Similarities and differences between religions are similarities and differences between cultures.

This correlation between religions and cultures is not accidental. It is in the nature of religions to embody representative cultural elements, so that, in a restricted but significant sense, a culture lives on in its religion. It is these cultural elements that confer on any particular religion its distinctive identity. A religion is a culture acting in a certain way, namely, attending to salvation.

This is not to assert that cultures and religions are simply identical. A culture is the *whole* way of life of a people. It may or may not be focused on salvation. A religion is a way of life focused on salvation. It is not a whole way of life.

Also, no causality is being asserted here. It is not as if cultures produced religions, or religions produced cultures. There is no way of establishing causality here in one direction exclusively. What is asserted is that cultures are intrinsic and integral parts of their religions. They are the diversifying factor. The variety of religions goes together with the variety of cultures.

The religions of Indian origin are religions of the self, and of liberation. Their aim is above all deliverance from the limitations of the empirical ego. The Buddhist is content with the practical achievement of this goal, the Hindu and the Jain postulate in addition a true self, of unending bliss. But all agree in their general perspective: the ego is something to be dismantled. The dominant feeling is a longing for release.

The religions of Chinese origin are religions of nature and of harmony. Man is a part of nature, and the way of nature is the way of man. The Confucian emphasises human nature, true humanity; the Taoist turns to cosmic nature; the Chinese Buddhist sees all in each and each in all, and the humanity of the absolute. But they agree in their overall perspective: nature is a harmonious whole, and we would do well to be in harmony with the nature of things.

The religions of Semitic origin are religions of morality and of God. The insistent claims of moral ideals, which govern the ways people treat one another, are personified in the will of one who is all-holy, who has revealed his will to men, and who will pass an irrevocable judgement on them. The Jew sees this will as applying in a special way to a particular people; the Christian emphasises man's weakness and God's power to save; the Muslim stresses the societal fulfilment of the will. But in their general outlook they agree: there is no evil greater than moral evil, and salvation lies in the will of God.

The same affinities between religions are reflected visibly in the functions and forms of their solemn places. Those of the Semitic religions are places of assemblage, meeting halls. Synagogue, church, and mosque are not gardens, or places of sacrifice, but places for a community to come together regularly. This is natural for religions giving such a central place to the way people relate to one another. Although many Christians consider the Eucharist celebrated in their churches a sacrifice, it does not follow that the offering of sacrifice is the main purpose of church buildings. To offer sacrifice you do not need a basilica: you need an altar, which can just as well be in the open air.

The solemn places of the East Asian religions are gardens: pavilions arranged among trees and shrubs, where tranquillity of spirit may be sought in contemplation. They are not at all places for a community to assemble. The identical description applies to Buddhist, Confucian, Taoist and Shinto shrines.

The solemn places of the religions of India are neither gardens nor assembly halls. From the Hindu temple, the Indian Buddhist stupa and the Jain temple, nature is excluded: the early temples were commonly caves, both temples and stupas are typically of rock. Though they may sometimes be crowded, they are not arranged for holding communal assemblies. They are places for individual sacrifice and remembrance, places of solitary worship, veneration and reverence.

Christianity has been classified here as a religion of Semitic origin. However it is only partly that. It is as much a mirror of the late Hellenistic world. For a brief period the peoples around the shores of the Mediterranean participated in a common culture, which fused into an exotic mixture the religious fervour of Egypt and Syria, the speculation and poetry of Greece, the learning of Alexandria, and the politics and many-ghettoed urbanisation of Rome. To the typical concerns of the Semitic religions Christianity added a preoccupation with mortality and a longing for eternal life, and a saviour who, like those of Egypt and Syria, dies and rises again. Its God had a *logos*, than which nothing could be more Greek. Its belief was decided, and partly still is, in the Roman fashion, a political decree imposing an end on speculation, by public authority.

Religions originating in any one culture are members of a family. The links between them are family relationships, and families of religions are distinct as cultures are distinct. The resemblances between members of a family are cultural resemblances. Whether the differences between them are cultural differences is a moot point. There are indications that this is the case. It is fairly clear in the case of the Semitic religions. Judaism, Christianity and Islam are evidently members of one family, yet the cultural differences are equally apparent. With the religions of Indian and Chinese origin it is not so clear. Hinduism, Jainism and Indian Buddhism are so profoundly akin, it may be that they should be viewed merely as currents of the same stream: Jainism as the inevitable unorthodoxy, Buddhism, which was so readily absorbed back into the fold of Hinduism, as its export variety. However there is some evidence to suggest that even here we are dealing with cultural differences. Orthodox Hinduism is the religion of that cultural compromise that issued from the Aryan invasions of the second millennium B.C., and their intermingling with the predominantly Dravidian population. While the earliest strata of the Vedas show us the elemental nature-worship typical of the Indo-Aryans everywhere (Greeks, Romans, Celts), the latest strata, in the Upanishads, proclaim a sublime and metaphysically sophisticated mysticism, which has remained the core of the Hindu tradition. In Jainism, however, we seem to encounter a voice out of the pre-Aryan past. This is the claim of the Jains themselves, in their tradition of the twenty-three Tirthankaras, and perhaps it should not be dismissed as lightly as it sometimes is. In addition, some important Jain conceptions are manifestly primitive: the higher self in man is thought of as material, and the sinful forces that defile it are physical qualities with distinct colours, and capable of being physically washed off. Buddhism, likewise, appears to have been of non-Aryan origin: Gautama's clan, for example, was apparently not of Aryan stock.[1]

The religions of Chinese origin may simply represent a sociological distinction, the Confucian tradition being urban and literate, and the Taoist rural. But the Chinese of the sixth century B.C. were a fusion of peoples, and there is good reason to believe that Taoism derives from the naturalistic Shang culture, while the Confucian tradition stems from the more moralistic culture of the Chou.[2]

The unity of a culture of any physical size is only

relative. Subcultures can almost always be found. To a visitor from another planet the human race would constitute one culture. Mankind itself tends to see its own differences more sharply, and is quick to scent the foreigner. To the extent that cultural differences prevail, even within what we would normally call a unified culture, we must expect corresponding differences of religion.

Just as one general culture may support different religions within its family, so one religion may inhabit different cultures. To the extent that it does, it tends to diversify into different religions, or at least into significantly different varieties of itself; it remains only partly the same religion.

The outstanding example of this is the career of Buddhism on leaving India and entering China. Indian Buddhism is a secure representative of Indian culture. Wherever the religion is to be found, as in Ceylon, that culture is to be found. But when it crossed the Himalayas it underwent a drastic change. In the end Chinese Buddhism has more in common with Taoism and Confucianism than it has with the Buddhism of India. This is clearest in the case of Ch'an, but it is also true of the T'ien T'ai, Hua Yen and Pure Land movements. They are novel Chinese creations. Their putative parent, the Mahayana, provided a stimulus, a suggestion. Chinese Buddhism is the heir of early Taoism, with devotional elements. Rightly understood, there is nothing in the Ch'an masters that is not already present in Chuang-Tzu. To the extent that it preserves its continuity, Buddhism in China is an extension of Indian culture; to the extent that it is different, the difference lies in Chinese culture.

45

A similar illustration is provided by the career of Christianity. Wherever Christianity has genuinely adopted, or been adopted by, a different culture, its identity has undergone a transformation. The first alteration occurred immediately it went down from the mountaintops of Jewish Palestine to the Greek-speaking coast: it was then transformed from a reform movement within Judaism to a Hellenistic mystery, a competitor of Isis and Mithra. When it reached Rome, it became a religion of authority and dogma. In North Africa it became Carthaginian: a religion of immolation and predestination. When it finally had taken root among the Germanic peoples of the north, it emerged as Protestantism.

Wherever it goes, it carries with it the culture of the first-century Mediterranean world. Equally, wherever it goes it changes into something new. The Christianity of America is not the Christianity of Europe except in so far as the culture of America is the culture of Europe. The Christianity of Africa cannot be the Christianity of Italy or England except in so far as the culture of Africa is theirs also. Similarly, the Judaism of America cannot be the Judaism of Israel, just as it cannot be the Judaism of the Yemeni. Where there is a different culture, to that extent there is a different religion.

Two particular features of religions seem to have no correlation with individual cultures. One is whether they are saviourist or pelagian; the other is their being national or universal in scope. In every major culture there is at least one religion centered on the figure of a saviour, and there are also pelagian ones; and in each culture there is at least one religion whose membership is restricted in principle or by the nature of the case to its own particular people, and there are also religions that hope to embrace the whole of mankind. It appears that any fundamental religious form seeks expression in all of these modes. Their universality suggests they may be as deeply rooted in human nature as the structure of religion itself.

A religion, on one level, is a habitual pattern of observable behaviour. From this aspect it can be viewed as a set of signs, a way of communicating, a language. On another level a religion consists in the unobservable patterns of interest that motivate and explain what can be observed. These interest patterns constitute the hidden rules governing the visible activity, the grammar of the language. On a third level there is the structure of religion as such, the system of those elements common to all religions and peculiar to none.

The structure of this third level derives from the primordial tension between the real and the ideal. The reality we experience is never ideal. Just by that fact it clamours for the ideal, as at once its negation and fulfilment. This tension is by no means purely conceptual, but above all practical: the ideal offers salvation from the real.

But this offer will be merely notional unless the ideal can become real. The tension between them demands that there be a path from here to there. Some event or chain of events must actualise the ideal. It is this salvific path or occurrence that transforms the merely ideal into salvation.

However, it is not obvious that salvation is possible. The experience of the real as unsatisfactory suggests the opposite. To establish the possibility of salvation, reality must be interpreted. Reality must be such that salvation is possible.

But again, the reality that makes salvation possible is not reality as it is ordinarily experienced. This, by definition in religion, is radically unsatisfactory. Salvific reality is hidden. In some way or other it must be disclosed.

These five elements, the unsatisfactoriness of ordinary experience, the contrasting ideal, the path from the one to the other, hidden reality and its disclosure, can be viewed as interrelated in different ways, but in one version or another they are common elements of religions, and must be considered necessary to the structure of religion as such.

Into this structure no elements distinctive of particular cultures enter. Given the initial step, the experience of reality as unsatisfactory, the structure unfolds of itself, by its own inner logic. But cultures have a great deal to say about how far that first step will be taken. Some cultures are favourable to the experiencing of reality as unsatisfactory, others tend to foster contentment with the world as we find it. An outstanding example of the first is the Indian, and of the second, the Chinese. By deciding this a culture decides in advance to what extent it will be propitious to the burgeoning of religion. In so far as the bitterness of reality is accepted or felt less sharply, the tug of the ideal slackens, expectations are moderated, the path to their attainment will be less drastic, the hidden reality they require has less need of transcendence, and the manner of its disclosure will be closer to hand. In short, the whole character of the enterprise is altered in the direction of the feasible. The result may only marginally justify the name religion. In general this description seems to apply to the Confucian tradition.

On this level, of the structure of religions as such,

cultures are significant to this extent, that they favour or discourage the existence of any religion whatever, the instantiation of the general nature and traits of religions as such. But it is beyond this level, in the particular structures of particular religions that cultures are distinctively embodied and live on, if in distilled or crystallised form, and confer identity. They do this both in the dimension of observable activity and of unobservable interests.

On the level of observable behaviour, a religion can be viewed as a set of signs. This is also true of a culture. What makes this behaviour, this set of signs religious is that it is focused on salvation. But for something to be focused on salvation, it must already exist. Religions do not create the signs they use out of nothing, they infuse new meaning into signs already present in their culture. They can only make use of a sign for their own purposes if it is already familiar and has meaning, that is, if it already exists within the culture. Christianity could place at its centre the image of a man on a cross because crosses with men on them were part of Roman culture. Moses could hear the voice of God in a burning bush because the idea of a God who might speak from burning bushes was already part of his mental environment.

This is not to say that it is impossible for a religion to invent a sign. It is just that it is not their business, as religions. The creation of signs is the work of cultures as cultures. The concern of religions is with salvation. If a novel sign is developed within a religion, that is a cultural event, not a religious one. The religious event takes place when the sign is made a sign of salvation.

The entire body of signs we find in a religion have their origin and derivation in a culture. What is decisive for the religion is the use made of the sign. The voice may be the voice of a religion, but the words are the words of a culture. To encounter the observable side of a religion is to encounter the sign system of a culture, that is, to encounter the culture itself in its observable dimension. Not merely accidentally, but essentially and inescapably, to encounter Hinduism is to encounter Indian culture, to encounter Taoism is to encounter Chinese culture, to encounter Islam is to encounter Arabic culture, and to encounter Christianity is to encounter that exotic amalgam which was late Hellenistic Roman culture.

The culture of a religion's origin is fundamental to it, but is not the only significant one in this regard. It has been pointed out above that every culture a religion enters effectively leaves its mark: if Judaism in New York is different from the Judaism of fifth-century Babylonia, it is because the culture of New York differs from the culture of fifth-century Babylonia.

It is not only in the sphere of the observable that this holds. It applies also, and more importantly, to that hidden realm of interest patterns which animates and governs the observable, the particular grammar of each particular religion. Above and beyond the basic pattern of interest and value common to all religions, each religion has its own unobservable but distinctive set of interests and values, which explain its characteristic manifest behaviour. Here we are no longer dealing with signs, but with interests and valuations that determine the use of signs in this particular religion as distinct from others. Where do these interests and values come from? Not from the nature of religion, or the basic structure of religion as such, for then they would be common to all religions. Are they the independent creation of the

religion's founders? No doubt religions generally owe
their characteristic emphasis in at least some measure to
the people who founded them. But it cannot be imagined
that the founders of religions stand outside their own
cultures. It is not as if a religion were ever founded by a
single individual. The emergence and development of a
religion requires the association and cooperation of
many, and the many are inevitably rooted in their
culture even when they are in revolt against it.

At this intermediate level the basic structure is still
present: the dominant interest or value is salvation. But
apart from this each religion has its own interests. The
configuration of interests around this centre differs with
each religion. A religion's interests are arranged among
themselves in a distinctive order; some values receive
greater emphasis or prominence than others. It is the
business of religions to focus life on salvation, and they do
this not only to the observable activities of life, but above
all to the hidden interests and values that motivate and
carry those activities. A religion marshals whatever
interests it finds and draws them into the service of
salvation. It is not possible to be interested solely in
salvation. By the nature of the case some interests will be
more susceptible to such service than others. But for any
interest or value to be drawn into the service of salvation
it must already be held as a value, it must be already
present as an interest. The centring of interests on
salvation does not of itself entail that interests equally
susceptible of such centring will be emphasised and
others neglected. Where this happens, where a religion
concentrates great attention on one value, and almost
wholly neglects another of equal claim—and this is true
at least of each of the major religions—this is a cultural

fact. An interest pattern representing a culture is drawn into the service of a religion, is embodied in the religion, so that, on this unobservable level also, the culture is crystallised and lives on in the religion.

From this it follows, not merely that a religion is part of a culture, which no one would dispute, but that the culture is part of the religion, an inseparable and essential part of it. Try as it may, a religion can never dissociate itself from its own culture, on pain of losing its identity. It is sometimes maintained that religions are too culture-laden, that they would be better able to secure a sympathetic hearing in lands now foreign to them if they abandoned the cultural baggage they carry, and presented their message in its original purity. What this overlooks is that the original message emanated from a culture and contains forever within itself the embodiment of that culture.

In their more traditional forms religions tend to recognise this, and to insist that a convert adopt their culture. Orthodox Judaism has insisted on using Hebrew, traditional Roman Catholicism on using Latin, Islam on using Arabic, in each case predicting disaster if the ancient language is abandoned. In general events have proved them astute judges. In this respect, as in some others, the religious conservative seems to have a better grasp of the nature of religion than the familiar species of liberal who reinterprets his tradition radically but claims it is the same. When the Muslim says the Koran cannot be translated, he is right. Arabic culture requires the Arabic language, and Arabic religion requires Arabic culture. When the Second Vatican Council was contemplating allowing the use of vernacular languages by Catholics in place of Latin, members of the

Jewish community warned it would be a mistake, and certainly in many places it has been: what sounded impressive with little effort in Latin appears in English as trite and superficial unless the celebrant utters it from the heart and goes to pains to speak it well—a combination that cannot be presumed to recur with great frequency. Meanwhile a bond of cultural unity has been broken. Abandonment of the language is a good part of abandonment of the culture, but in the long run the attempt frustrates itself: the culture is built into the religion, and it cannot abandon itself. The result has often been merely an increase in dissatisfaction.

Not only is its culture of origin an integral part of a religion; a religion *is* a culture, from a particular aspect. A religion is a way of life focused on salvation. A culture is the entire way of life of a people. In its surface structure, a culture consists in the whole set of habitual patterns of a group's observable behaviour. In its hidden structure it is the complete configuration of interests that characterises the group. It follows that a religion, on both levels, is not something distinct from its culture, but an aspect of the culture, is the culture itself acting in a certain way, namely, seeking salvation.

What do we gain by this observation, that to encounter a religion is to encounter a culture? What does it imply?

One way to bring this out is by contrast. We would not say that to encounter a science is to encounter a culture. One science, say chemistry, does not differ from another, say physics, in virtue of cultural differences. It is not that biology embodies one culture, and astronomy a different culture. The sciences by their nature cut across cultures. The laws of the state may differ in Russia and America, but the laws of physics do not. Even science as a whole, in contrast to, say, business or politics, while it may constitute a realm of special endeavour, does not incorporate, let alone constitute, a particular culture.

The statement, 'to encounter a religion is to encounter a culture', means that to encounter a religion is always to encounter more than a religion. In general it suggests that the principles that apply to cultures will apply, *mutatis mutandis*, to religions. Some of these are:

Cultures are distinguished not only by thinking different thoughts and performing different actions, but also by entertaining significantly different feelings. They encourage different sensibilities, and conjure up different emotions. This affective load is carried over into the sphere of religion, and alters not only what, but how, things are approached and reacted to. It is often overlooked that different religions foster characteristically different feelings.

A culture is defined by its past. It is not just any pattern of activity, but a habitual and traditional one, one that has taken root among a people. It is not the habitual activity of a solitary individual, but the established customs of a society. An inevitable and necessary feature of all cultures, therefore, is stability or inertia. They tend not to change. A culture is never only skin deep; it is tenacious, it has a firm hold on those who have been formed by it. Once acquired, it can never be wholly thrown off. The leaving of one's native culture for a different one is an act that shakes the foundations of the individual's personality and threatens to undermine his identity. Cultures have an astonishing persistence, in the individual and in society.

This tenacity, this rooted persistence, is equally a feature of religions. A biologist can become a physicist, a mathematician become a logician, without psychological strain. His personality is not necessarily threatened or his identity uprooted. But for a Jew to become a Christian, or a Christian a Muslim, is a very different thing. That is to abandon a whole way of life, to attempt to throw off one's former identity, and acquire a new personality. Understandably it never happens fully, and rarely even partially. It is for good reason that most people die in the religion they were born in.

The true reality of a culture is not directly observable. It does not lie in the manifest activity of the group, but in the hidden patterns of interest that govern the manifest. A culture is distinguished by what it habitually values. Ideas and beliefs, at least so far as they are formulated and shared, belong to the surface of the culture, its manifest and observable dimension; they are part of the language by which the group communicates. Like the rest of this language they are governed by the invisible grammar of values at the heart of the culture. The distinctive thing about a culture is not a set of opinions, but a set of interests relatively unified. Its opinions may change drastically: if its configuration of interests is preserved, the culture is preserved. In cultures, interest has primacy over opinion, value, in a broad sense, over truth. Its constellation of interests decides what the culture will pay attention to and neglect, and so what it will think or not think, as well as what it will do or not do.

Similarly, the true reality of a religion is not directly observable. The real religion is not its manifest activity, but the set of interests that govern the visible activity. When we are dealing with a religion, we are dealing before all else with a set of interest patterns. But the interest patterns distinctive of particular religions are the interest patterns of cultures. Therefore commitment to a particular religion's way of life is a commitment to the interests of a particular culture. What appears as the incompatibility of different religious ways of life is the mutual exclusiveness of different cultural interests. To maintain the superiority of one religion to another, i.e. of one way of living focused on salvation to another, is to maintain the superiority of one culture to another, i.e. of one set of cultural values to another.

The beliefs of a religion belong to its surface structure, its manifest and observable dimension; they are part of the language by which it communicates, and like the rest of this language they are governed by the invisible grammar of values at the heart of the religion. In religions, belief is subordinate to interest, theory to the requirements of practice, cognition to volition, fact to value. The doctrines of a religion may change dramatically: if its distinctive pattern of interests is preserved, the religion is preserved. Interest directs attention to certain aspects of the world and neglects others. But the invisible grammar of values at the heart of a religion is the grammar of values at the heart of a culture. The interest patterns distinctive of particular religions are the interest patterns of cultures. Therefore, the adoption of a particular religious faith is in the first instance the adoption of a set of cultural interests. Commitment to a particular creed is commitment to a set of cultural values. To assert the truth of Islam is to assert the superiority of the cultural values of seventh-century Arabia, just as to practise yoga is to defend and embody the values of Indian culture, and to celebrate the Eucharist is to commit oneself to the cultural values of the late Hellenistic Mediterranean world.

What appear to be conflicts between religious faiths must be seen, then, first and foremost as conflicts between cultural values. An ecumenical movement towards the peaceful coexistence or the synthesis of religious faiths constitutes primarily a movement towards the peaceful coexistence and the synthesis of cultural values. The elaboration of a theology is the justification of a set of cultural values. The emergence of a new religion awaits the emergence of a new culture.

# 3 Contingency

The general truth of the contingency of religions may be illustrated from a different aspect in three particular operations that have played a prominent role in their development: the habitation, migration, and fusion of ideal conceptions.

1. Our lives take shape under the impact of the contradictoriness of things. We are constantly thrust against the jagged edges of contrasts, oppositions and incompatibilities: the well-intended action ends in disaster, the life of one is the death of another no less good; in the long run we cannot tell what will be for good and what for ill; everything meets with resistances. It is by no means obvious that things have to be this way. The refractory character of experience clamours for explanation.

One kind of solution that has had a steady vogue consists in dividing up the universe itself, the totality of things, into opposed and contradictory halves, declaring one half to be unacceptable and without value, and bestowing high favour and privilege on the other half. The products of this feat may be labelled 'cosmic dualism'. Three forms of this operation have been especially prominent, and each has enjoyed a special blessing in a particular culture, a particular human place and time.

One is to make a cleft between the world of appearance or experience on the one side, and the contrasting world of reality on the other. Appearance is not to be confused with Truth; the gap between them is starkly highlighted, indeed a chasm is opened between them. The world of ordinary experience is not, in the last analysis, real; reality and truth lie beyond it. Only what is permanent is real; what is merely temporary and fleeting is insubstantial. The universe our senses report possesses endless variety and insistent multiplicity, but Truth is One. Ordinary experience is therefore at bottom delusion, and salvation consists in being freed from this delusion, in seeing and thereby ascending into the single oneness of Being. This accomplishment may be labelled 'mystical dualism'. (One variety of it is commonly termed 'non-dualism' on the grounds that it is not appropriate to call the connection between the absolute and the relative either a unity or a duality, but that is beside the present point.) This cosmic cleavage has occurred sporadically in various places and times, but historically it has found a uniquely warm welcome and a uniquely permanent home in one place, India.

A second operation goes at the business of cutting the world up into contradictory halves by drawing a line, which turns out to be a battle line, between the good on the one hand, and the wicked on the other. There is the side of right, and there is the side of wrong. There is the camp of the just, and the camp of the unjust. There are the sons of light, and the sons of darkness. Between these two camps an everlasting war is waged. But conveniently it is possible to desert, or be converted, to move from one side to the other, and salvation consists in doing just that, in transferring oneself from the camp of the wicked to that of the good. Since there is an understandable tendency for whoever is speaking at the moment to conceive of his own side as 'the good', salvation usually means leaving 'them' to join up with 'us'. This is moral dualism; its historical home was the Persia of Zoroaster, and perhaps its most remarkable monument the Behistun Inscription of Darius.[1]

There is a third sort of dualism which carves the universe into opposing realms by applying the moral categories of the second to the mystical categories of the first. Typically it has held that matter and the body are evil, and spirit is good. The world of experience, of the senses, is wicked; the realm of the good can be discovered only by leaving the body behind. Salvation consists in cleansing oneself of the body with its innate defilement, and rising to the sphere of the spirit. This may be designated 'metaphysical dualism'. Its home was the Hellenistic Mediterranean, and its classic exposition is in the philosophy of Plotinus.

An interesting point is that the political implications of these dualisms are very diverse. For mystical dualism the world of politics is uninteresting, it is merely part of the world of illusion. Mystical dualism therefore poses no threat to any ruling power, and is also useless to it. Moral dualism, by contrast, is a natural ideology for any who desire to seize or preserve power. Those who are on our side are good, those opposed to us are evil. Our enemies are not merely in error, mistaken or misguided, they are wicked. Every war becomes a war of the sons of light against the sons of darkness. Politics is the battleground of good and evil. The tendency of metaphysical dualism is just the opposite, to be subversive of authority, for since the body is evil, and everyone has a body, including those in authority, they are to that extent evil and not to be trusted. Those who would be pure must resist the impositions of civil government. A population of this persuasion settled especially in an arc stretching through northern Spain, the south of France and northern Italy, and up the valley of the Rhone, providing a fertile ground of reform movements over a millenium. The Priscillianists, the Cathari and Albigenses resisted established authority in the name of the spirit. Although it was not adopted into official Christianity, it made a profound and lasting impression on it.

Cosmic dualisms can be interpreted as attempts to cope with the devastating ambiguities of experience by negating and rejecting a substantial portion of it. There are some responses to the ambiguity of life that are not dualistic in this cosmic sense. A notable one is the Chinese approach familiar in the notions of yin and yang. The written character for yin appears to have originally represented a cloud hovering over the earth, or perhaps the shady side of a mountain, and that for yang the shining sun, or the side of a mountain exposed to the sun. From this perspective each individual thing is compounded of two contrasting elements, one variously represented as active, male, bright, dry, the other receptive, female, shadowlike, moist. In early Taoism at least, neither of these elements is regrettable in itself. For the Tao Te Ching or Chuang Tzu, it is not that yang is morally good, for instance, while yin is morally bad: both are necessary, and necessary for each other. The contrast and opposition we experience in life arise by their interaction, but what we experience as opposition is more appropriately seen as harmony. It is not that one half of the cosmos is yin and the other half yang: the location of the contrast is transferred from the universe to particular things. It is not that some things are yin and others yang, but everything contains both, in varying degrees. Their natural association is a harmony of opposites. Chinese thinking is not natively dualistic in the cosmic sense used here; it is no coincidence that it is also not notably problematic, in the sense that it has not tended to feel as acutely and intensely as other cultures that life as such and fundamentally is a problem, that there is something essentially out of joint about it. Such an idea scarcely occurs in Chinese literature, the nearest thing to it commonly being a poignant awareness that all things pass away.

A case can be made that Jewish thinking in the rabbinic tradition is not dualistic, despite the heavy influence of the moral dualism of Persia on Semitic culture in general, and on the earlier religion of Israel. But the rabbinic schools, in a traditional hostility to philosophy, never developed any theory to account for the ambiguities of experience, preferring to deal with them existentially, by means of stories, and so they offer no systematic or conceptual alternative.

2. In the sixth century before the Christian era two Persian kings, Cyrus and Darius, putting in some overtime on horseback, assembled an empire larger, more various and better organised than any seen before. It was in fact the first genuine empire we know of, in the sense of a truly multinational state, and the world was duly impressed. Wealthy Greek Asia Minor, cultured, declining Egypt, once-powerful Babylon and Assyria, and even a portion of northern India of the sages were drawn into a common fate, contributed to a common

army, and were united for trade by a network of roads. A canal was dug through Suez, and Persian ships visited Italy and Sicily. Heraclitus and Second Isaiah lived at one end, at the same time that the Buddha was preaching somewhat to the east of the other end. This unification of peoples so diverse and till then so remote from one another, this sudden breaking down of national boundaries in a vast supernation, was eventually to demand a new kind of religion, and also to create an enduring symbol for it.

Emperors being new on the scene, there was no ready name for them, and Darius therefore styled himself 'the King of Kings'. It is true, the power of the Persian emperors had surprising weaknesses: when they wanted to move from their summer residence in Ecbatana to their winter residence in Susa across the Zagros mountains, they had to pay tribute on occasion to the mountain tribesmen. But such weaknesses were unimportant. What counted was the appearance. The Persian emperors created an *image* of what a really great ruler, a ruler of the nations, a ruler who could break the kings of the earth, would look like. It was an image of unsurpassed baroque magnificence. Absolute authority, maintained solely by force, and susceptible to force, found its appropriate reflection in a picture, not alone of classical restraint and simplicity, but also of a splendour that smacked of the decadent and barbaric.

Some of this splendour can be reconstructed from the reliefs at Persepolis, the capital built to be the symbolic pinnacle of the empire. The front wall of the *Apadana*, a sort of raised and open reception hall, portrays the procession of the nations at the New Year's Festival: the twenty-three subject peoples, from India to Egypt and

Ephesus, in their national costumes, bearing signs of their submission, with the King of Kings seated on a *sedes gestatoria* being carried on their shoulders in a manner somewhat reminiscent of the pope in St Peter's. The architecture of Persepolis is equally illuminating: rows of stately Greek columns, standing however not on Greek pedestals, but on bases cut to resemble the lotus blossom, and ending at the top not in any of the classic Greek capitals, but in the most ornate and sumptuous decorations, one piled on top of the other. The columns taper sublimely towards heaven, but the heaven they reach has an air of mystical luxury. The whole has a strangely mixed effect, combining a sheer glorying in power with a lofty idealism.

Historians tell us that this Persian monarchy was extinguished by the Greeks, when Alexander put Persepolis to the torch. But alas for military victories which bring peoples into such close contact that they begin to perceive advantages in the other's way of doing things, and practically guarantee that, whichever side is victorious, it will by that very fact succumb at least partially to the culture it has opposed. As soon as Alexander was master of the Persian empire, he lost no time in donning his enemy's imperial robes, putting the Persian's crown on his own head and proclaiming himself that gentleman's successor. Alexander became a Persian.

The Persian domains were consciously Hellenised, and the Hellenic domains were unconsciously Persianised. Not only did Persian dress become the fashion, Persian administration the form of government, a Persian god, Mithra, subsequently take over the Roman army and guilds of Roman merchants—one of the initiation degrees in the Mithraic cult was 'Persian', even when the

Persians were the enemy—but especially the Persian monarch, that king of kings, became the model of supreme power.

The Persian way of thinking was authoritarian and arbitrary, handled large distances readily, was fairly well organised, thought on a grand scale, and was intensely religious in a rather vague way. This mentality diffused itself throughout the Mediterranean. The ideals of Greek democracy sank beneath its waves. The image of the Persian monarchy preserved its fascination and was handed on. Sometimes this image is referred to as the 'Oriental Despot'. But it is not the picture of any Chinese emperor, or even of any Indian prince. It is in fact a thoroughly Indo-European creation, and it duly migrated westward, among its own. From Alexander it was inherited by the emperors of Rome. Darius had no more faithful heir than Constantine, the first Christian emperor, who established his legacy securely in his new capital on the Bosporus. Eusebius of Caesarea has left us a moving account of how the Christian bishops felt when, newly released from persecution and concealment, they found themselves summoned to council at Constantine's palace: God on high sat on his heavenly throne, surrounded by his royal court, and Constantine was his representative. Constantine was the new Cyrus and the new Alexander.[2] Five centuries later, in the midst of Europe's darkness, the image was still vivid and flourishing in the figure of Charlemagne, the new Constantine, founder of the new Rome and the new Constantinople.[3] If we look for the present heir of the image, we may find him, I think, in the basilica of St Peter's, still carried in procession on his throne, and wafted by an occasional breeze from the same tall ostrich fans.

The point of recounting the story of this image is that it has had a profound influence on the highest conceptions of Western religion. It is important to remember that it combines immense splendour with absolute authoritarianism. Already in the New Testament it is applied to Christ: he is 'the King of Kings'. It was no mean feat, to impose Darius's royal robes on Jesus of Nazareth, who had taught his followers not to resist evil, and rode on an ass. But the idea was taken up with the greatest enthusiasm by his followers. In the Middle Ages Christ the King quite supplanted Christ the suffering servant, and as recently as 1925 a special feast day was instituted in honour of Christ the King. When Christians think of Christ, what they have in mind often enough is a figure of baroque majesty that still betrays its origin in the audience halls of Persepolis.

The influence of this image has gone further. It is the ordinary man's notion of God. No doubt the ordinary man may have various notions of God, not necessarily in intimate harmony with one another. But one of them, and an important one, one that gives him much encouragement and consolation, is that of a king, and a king of kings, enthroned on high in sumptuous splendour, ministered to by his court of angels, the world his footstool. He conquers his enemies, to him belongs victory, he will avenge, he will rule his enemies with a rod of iron and break them like potsherds. It is an image of majesty and glory; it is also an image of inferior morality. It is splendid, and it is barbarous.

The notion is not to be confused with that of the king's divinity. Many peoples have looked upon their kings as divine. That is a way of viewing kings, but this is a way of viewing God. Instead of telling us to see the king as

67

divine, it tells us to picture divinity as if it were a king.

The influence of this image has not been restricted to the popular imagination. It is enshrined in the official and classic theologies of the West. The God of Western theology is one of blood and battles, he delights in receiving praise, is quick to take offence, and minute, even petty, in exacting punishment. The penalty for disobeying him is condemnation to everlasting torture. The God of Judaism slaughters the Egyptians and the Canaanites, and will not let Moses, his friend, enter the Promised Land because on one occasion his faith had faltered. The God of Christianity will have his wrath appeased, or his honour satisfied, only by the blood sacrifice of his own Son. Jesus insists that we forgive others without limit, for if we do not God will punish us with everlasting fire! The God of Islam 'has prepared fetters and chains and a blazing fire for the unbelievers', and on the day of judgement will reign supreme. The reward of his loyal follower is to become a courtier at the royal throne. He is the ultimate authoritarian personality. To worship this God is to worship power.

Not only has the image of the Persian monarch inspired the West's theologies, it has also profoundly influenced its philosophical conceptions. The supreme reality is infinite power, the absolute is absolute authority: not only the moral power of the ideal, or the inner authority of wisdom and goodness, but first the power of sheer brute physical force, for this is required to create being out of nothing. Being itself is power, Plato said. It is not true that Athens has nothing to do with Jerusalem. Both were impressed by the majestic figure on the throne.

It has happened before, as we shall have occasion to note, and it has now happened again, that we have attained the anomalous position of having higher standards for ourselves than we attribute to our God. In the past this has led to improvements in our notion of God; a similar task awaits us now.

3. The creation of the Persian empire had a further effect. Up to that time the only religions in existence in the Middle East and round the Mediterranean were tribal, ethnic, or national, the particular religions of particular peoples. The Egyptians had Egyptian religion, the Babylonians Babylonian religion, the Greeks had Greek religion, the Jews Jewish religion. But with the appearance of a political unit embracing a large number of peoples and a great variety of religions from India to Egypt and Greece, and with the building of roads and the development of trade to intermingle and bring them up against one another without traditional hostilities, an awareness spread gradually of the need for a less nationally restricted kind of religion. A new type of religion was required, one that would be not just for one nation or people, but for all mankind. After the initial revolts within the Persian empire had been put down, some 200 years of peace prevailed in the Middle East. But the national gods had derived much of their utility and popularity from the necessities of war. When war declined, national identities diminished in importance, and so did the national gods and religions. There was a new experience of the unity of mankind, and it called for a god and a religion that would be, at least in principle and scope, not less than universal.

The religion of the Persians themselves was quite unable to fill this need. It was distinctly a religion for Persians, and Cyrus and Darius and their successors had the good sense never even to suggest to their subject peoples that they adopt it. The new kind of religion would have to be sought elsewhere, or created.

Roughly at the same time another development of like magnitude for religion was taking place. Death, the fact of death, the prospect of death, was becoming an object of paramount concern. For the tribal religions death had been merely a regrettable fact of life, to be warded off as long as possible, and then to be accepted. Religion existed to secure well-being. After death some shadowy kind of existence continued, no doubt, but if it was nothing unbearable, it was also nothing to look forward to. The Israelite after death would go down to She'ol, a world of shadows, where he would not be particularly happy, but also not particularly in pain. The Greek would go down to a similar place, Hades, to live as a shade among shades. It was a pity, but there it was. The Egyptians were rather more worried about what would happen to them after death. They had decided it was likely not to be so simple, and there would probably be a judgement. They would find themselves before Osiris, giving an account of themselves. There would be punishment for the wicked, and reward for the good. The Egyptian Book of the Dead, as it is called, is a lengthy and generally unconvincing protestation of complete and total innocence: I never killed anyone, I never robbed anyone, I never blasphemed against the Gods, I never told a lie, etc. But no one, not even the Egyptians, had suggested that the life to come was more significant, let alone more desirable, than the present life.

About four centuries before the Christian era, around the middle of the Persian period, this state of affairs began to change. The feeling spread that death is absurd, and since life must end in death, life is meaningless and weary. Death must be overcome. Not only new life was needed—that had always been felt—but immortality.

This preoccupation with death and immortality was not new. It had been cast into marvellous, moving poetry in the epic of Gilgamesh, perhaps three thousand years before the Christian era. Gilgamesh is an extrovert, a warrior, not given to deep thought, until his closest friend Enkidu dies, a fighter like himself, who had fought first against him and then alongside him, till that special bond existed between them which is reserved for men who have saved one another's lives. Gilgamesh had exulted in life and had never taken death very seriously. Now he sees that it threatens to drain the meaning out of life. What is the point of living, when you know you are going to die? It is intolerable that men should die, should cease, should merely end. Seeking some preventive against death, some medicine of immortality, he goes on a long and arduous journey, only to have his quest frustrated just as he seems to have attained his goal. Mankind must continue to die, and the fact will remain unbearable.

For long this sense of the outrageousness of death and this longing for immortality remained only an obscure current of feeling among the people of the Middle East. So long as the immortality sought was merely a prolongation of this present life, the desire for it was evidently futile. But a decisive change took place when a more stirring notion of the afterlife became current. This new idea was signalled in the preaching of Zoroaster to the Persian nobility that the destiny of man after death was not a world of shadows, but paradise. After death the good would receive an eternal reward in the House of Song, they would live with God in an existence by no

71

means less real than the present, and far more desirable. No doubt there were conditions attached, a bridge had to be crossed, a judgement had to be gone through, and perhaps one would fail and fall into the enduring misery of the House of the Lie. But with one stroke the life after death becomes more significant than this present life. The balance has shifted, the scales have gone down on the other side. The world to come is more important than this world. Now death has truly been overcome. It is merely a gate to life. In death 'life is but changed, not taken away'.

When these currents mingled, the growing sense for the unity of mankind arising out of the experience of empire, and the positive desire for the next world, overcoming the threat of death, there emerged a new kind of religion, quite different from the ancient civic religions. The new religions shared three novel features: they were universal in scope, open in principle to all nations, rather than to the members of but one;[4] the salvation they offered was not worldly welfare, or a rejuvenation of earthly life, but a blessed immortality hereafter; and they were intensely personal, instead of being the official activity of a civil society. The last of these was a consequence of the first two. The larger the group, the more alone the individual. A member of a clan or tribe is in some sense never alone; an inhabitant of a great city is anonymous. A religion for all men leaves the individual solitary. The universalisation of religion therefore was at the same time an individualising and a personalising of it. Also, dying is something the individual does by himself.

These new movements are usually referred to as mystery religions. Some of the better-known centre round such figures as Orpheus, Dionysus, Mithra, Attis,

Cybele, Isis, Serapis, and Sabazius. A mystery in this sense is not a puzzle, as when we speak of mystery stories; the term comes from a Greek verb, to initiate. In the case of a tribal or national religion one obtains membership in the religion by the simple expedient of being born into the tribe or nation. But with a universal religion membership can be obtained only through personal choice. It was a novel feature of the new religious movements that you could not be born into them, you had to be initiated into them.

The new movements promised to fulfil a deep religious need. But in two important respects they were sadly deficient. For one thing, they were obviously founded on myths. In a world coming to esteem historical fact, their stories could be set only in the once-upon-a-time of the fairy tale. Amid a growing desire for accurate knowledge and even abstract metaphysical truth, they could offer only stories, absorbing stories, but clearly tall stories. Secondly, and fatally, the divine figures they lavished attention on were not notably inspiring from a religious viewpoint. They were not distinguished by nobility of character. The highest achievement of Dionysus, for example, who figures prominently in the mysteries, seems to have been the invention of wine. This feat should by no means be underrated: but it scarcely elevates him to the pinnacle of holiness. The story is told of him that, attacked by pirates in the course of a sea voyage to Naxos, he turned them into dolphins. This betrays a regrettable petulance. From a moral standpoint Dionysus and his fellow deities in the mysteries were mediocre, representing no advance on the standards of their time; in fact they lagged considerably behind them. Socrates would not have turned an attacking pirate into a porpoise; he would have tried to turn him into a better man.

The mystery religions answered to deep longings of the spirit, but they lacked a symbolism sufficiently convincing to the mind and adequately impressive to the moral sense. Where could such a figure be found?

A profoundly impressive moral character was available in the Jewish God, Yahweh. He was a figure of unswerving righteousness and of the utmost nobility, totally dedicated to justice. Holy, he demanded holiness of men. From our vantage point in the twentieth century we may say that he had his faults, he was intolerant of competition, and especially he was addicted to the use of force as a solution for problems. But to the Mediterranean world these only enhanced his attractiveness. The universe, like the turbulent empire, needed a strong ruler. Morally and religiously the Jewish God towered above the deities around him. Of unlimited wisdom, goodness, and power, insistently just, but also merciful and loving; his greatness was such that no being could be imagined greater, Anselm was still to claim a millennium later.

But there was a difficulty. This God was the God of one particular people, and though they considered him sole Lord of the universe and of all men, they displayed a reluctance to share him. He had singled them out for special attention, he was their God and they were his people. He had given them a Law to live by, and this Law was by no means some set of general principles that could be adopted by anybody; it set up a specific way of living from day to day, filled with intricate custom. To become his client and worshipper meant adopting this Law and obeying it, that is, it meant becoming a Jew. At this prospect the other peoples of the Mediterranean were inclined to balk, and the Jews did not go to extraordinary lengths to encourage them.

However, a version of Judaism appeared on the scene that contained a radical internalisation of the Law. True obedience to God, and true disobedience, were of the heart and mind. What mattered was a person's inner attitude towards God and other men. The external observances imposed by the Law were pronounced of only secondary weight, and the customs enjoined additionally by the rabbis were unimportant. Murder and adultery could be committed adequately in the mind, it was no great thing to break the Sabbath because of hunger, and if your heart was in the right place the dietary rules could be safely neglected. Jesus's goal was a thoroughly spiritualised religion. He wished to refashion Judaism, not kill it. However, if his programme had been adopted, there can be little doubt that would have been the effective outcome. Also, although it may not be strictly logical, it has not been uncommon for Jews to feel that the end of the Jewish religion would bring the end of the Jewish people. In Judaea this proposal met with resistance.

Beyond the borders of Palestine, however, Jesus's version of Judaism had much to commend it. By spiritualising and internalising Judaism, Jesus had made possible its conversion to a mystery religion. At a price, Jesus had made the Jewish God available, at least in principle, to the rest of mankind.

One element was still missing. It was a great point in favour of the mystery religions that they promised victory over death. The Judaism of the Torah had not done this. Nevertheless this gap was already on its way towards being filled in Jewish circles. The Pharisees as a group believed in a resurrection of the dead. The message that Jesus himself had risen from the dead was the last piece needed to complete the picture. A Hellenised Pharisee and Roman citizen, Saul of Tarsus, grasped the situation, and in his hands the new religion of Christianity was born, Judaism transformed into a mystery religion. For the Law the person of Jesus himself was substituted. Attachment to the Hebrew law had required adoption into the Hebrew people. Attachment to the person of Jesus dissolved the Law, and provided a concrete focus for the new, expanded chosen people.[5]

What is to be learnt from these forays into the places and times and migrations of some religious ideals? That an idea requires special circumstances before it can make its entrance onto the stage of history says nothing about its validity. The geometry of Euclid and the equations of Maxwell required equally complex and equally fortuitous preparations, but they are not thereby proved false. An ideal is not discredited because it is not lived up to; similarly its validity must not be confused with its emergence. But, as contrasted with ideas in general, in the case of religious ideals the issue is more complicated, since it is often not so much a question of simple truth or falsity, as a question about the most appropriate or most adequate way to interpret life and the world. Also, it is a far cry from the isolated dawning of an ideal on an individual, to its transformation into a massive historical force in the embodiment of a religion. The emergence of a religious ideal in this sense is not only made possible, but also restricted, by the historical development of its culture. Thus the progressive refinement of religious perspective marches in step with the general elevation of thought and feeling, not as isolated qualities of individuals, but as features of the culture at large. The appropriateness of a religious ideal, and so its reasonableness, is rooted in its time and place, and must be judged within the context of their conditions.

# 4 Reflection

To their adherents all forms of religion appear reasonable. We may assume no one thinks himself unreasonable. But to the onlooker an air of irrationality hangs over all religion, and over some forms of it to an extreme degree. The best of religion gives the impression of a profound reflection on the nature of things. Yet the dedicated pursuit of reflection has often ended in the abandonment of religion.

If we survey the manifestations of religion in regard to the role reflection plays in them, we are confronted with an extreme diversity. Contrast:

the ritual of a Zen tea ceremony, and of Tennessee snake handling

the ecstasy of a Voodoo trance, and of St Teresa of Avila

a sermon by a fundamentalist faith healer, and by a liberal theologian

the meditations of the Tao Te Ching, and the fortune-telling in a Taoist temple

the Upanishads, and the Kalipuja

Aquinas, and the bleeding statue of Manayunk, Philadelphia.

The extremes of this diversity justify us in making at least a preliminary distinction between popular religion and reflective religion. The terms are self-explanatory, but elusive of definition.

79

To preclude misunderstandings: the distinction is not between traditions, as if Christianity were a reflective religion and Islam a popular one, for example. It cuts across traditions: in principle any religious tradition can appear in both popular and reflective forms.

Also, the distinction of itself is not evaluative, but only descriptive: it is an attempt to point to a phenomenon, it does not imply that one is 'better' than the other. Whether that is the case, or in what sense, is another question.

By 'reflection' here I mean the raising of questions about one's own belief or conduct previously unquestioned. The emphasis is on questioning, though not all questioning is reflection. Questioning of someone else's views may express merely an unreflective dogmatism. The same is true of questions occupied solely with future action, e.g., shall I go to the bank today or tomorrow? which do not put into question present belief or conduct. Reflection is the questioning of one's own assumptions.

To question is to doubt, to consider other possibilities and to wonder whether they may not be right. The question may remain unanswered. The initial viewpoint is not necessarily rejected: it may be retained as a belief, only it is then viewed with greater detachment. Instead of simply assuming or 'knowing' it is right, I believe it to be right. I am now aware of other possibilities as serious contenders, as conceivable alternatives: I believe it to be so, but conceivably it is otherwise. Reflection means envisaging alternatives to one's own assumptions.

In the absence of reflection first impressions are taken for truth, and that goal is adopted which suggests itself earliest. Thought and action are dominated by the impress of naïve appearance, the haste of instinct, and the momentum of tradition. The impact of reflection on any undertaking is in the direction of reasonableness.

What does it mean to be reasonable? The reasonableness of a belief is not decided by its content, but by its foundation. A belief is reasonable when it is supported by adequate grounds. Grounds are adequate when provided by the best evidence available. But the availability of evidence is relative to the historical situation, whether of the person holding the belief or of others judging it. Thus in principle any belief *can* be reasonable. In the sixteenth century it was widely believed that, since walnuts look like brains, eating walnuts must be good for the brain. The reasoning was based on a principle of analogy, that like fosters like.[1] In the absence of scientific method this was probably the best that could be done. In the sixteenth century the belief was reasonable: in the twentieth it would generally not be. This is to say that reasonableness is primarily not a quality of propositions, but of persons. It depends on the way the belief is arrived at, and the way it is held. It is people who are reasonable or unreasonable in their beliefs.

Sometimes we speak of people being reasonable in reference to a particular issue, as holding a particular belief; sometimes in reference to their overall behaviour, as a character trait. In this latter case reasonableness is a habit of basing one's opinions on grounds, and of being willing to change an opinion when confronted with weightier grounds. In this sense reasonableness is a virtue.

Thus the notions of reasonableness and truth do not entail one another. A belief may be reasonable but false, and unreasonable but true. Also, of two alternative beliefs, one may be less probable than the other, but still reasonable.

A parallel account can be given of the reasonableness of actions.

Rationality is not always the same thing as reasonableness. We use the term rational in a number of senses. In one sense a thing is rational when it has its origin in the activity of reasoning. In this sense music and dancing are never rational, though they may be thoroughly reasonable.

In another sense we say a thing is rational when we believe there is an explanation for it: it has causes, for example, and to the extent those causes are discovered, it can be understood. Art, the workings of the unconscious mind, and the life of the emotions are sometimes said to have 'a logic of their own'. If this implied the existence of competitive formal logics the statement would be misleading. What it usually means is that if we look hard enough we can find out why the thing happens. In this sense it is rational for a paranoid to commit murder: it is not an act out of the blue, there are forces at work that can explain it. That does not make it reasonable, only intelligible.

These two senses of 'rational' are descriptive, not evaluative. There is a third sense of the word that is synonymous with 'reasonable': the action or belief rests on grounds, and is justifiable. In this sense it is evaluative, a term of approval.

Whether religion is rational, then, will depend on what we mean by the question. In one sense it is never rational, in that its roots do not lie at all in the activity of reasoning, but in the experience of an imperative need. It does not draw its nourishment from theoretical considerations. It is not motivated by curiosity. From first to last it is practical. Its aim is not conceptual satisfaction, but salvation. A toothache may quickly become a concept, but before that it is an experience clamouring for action. The well-spring of religion is the experience that in some respect life is like a toothache. Let the philosopher try to understand man—the task of religion is to save him.

In another sense religion is always rational, in that we assume there are always reasons for it. It has causes, and to the extent those causes are discovered, it can be understood. In this sense religion is rational in the way it is rational for a psychotic to shoot people. There is an explanation for it. That does not make it justifiable, only intelligible.

In a third sense religion is variously rational, depending on the extent to which it is pervaded by reflective thought. No conscious activity is ever wholly reflective, or wholly unreflective. To the extent reflection is absent, the concrete forms of religion, both in thought and action, are guided by such factors as custom, emotion and appearance.

Thought is present in religion in a variety of ways. Sometimes it is merely concomitant with activity, such as ritual; sometimes it is given conceptual form in language; and sometimes it is subsumed into a higher silence. When a rain dance is being performed, or the cathedral chapter is singing matins, some measure of thought may be charitably presumed to accompany the action, at least from time to time. When an Australian aborigine tells the story of the Bagad-jimbiri, how they came up over the horizon and created the objects in the world by naming them, when the Council of Constantinople agrees on its statement of faith, or Shankara composes his treatise on the Brahmasutra, thought emerges explicitly in its own conceptual mode of expression, language. When a yoga adept or voodoo devotee enters into trance, when the Buddha refuses to answer questions and his follower retreats altogether from language, when Aquinas puts down his pen, judging theology to be straw, conceptual thought and language is taken up into something beyond itself, abandoned yet preserved, in a silence not only exterior but also interior: thought is fulfilled in the cessation of thought. In any of these modes religious thought can be more or less reflective.

The main topics of religious thought are given with the nature of religion: deliverance, the need for it, the path to it, the hidden reality that makes it attainable, and the disclosure of that reality. For popular religion these topics are of the utmost importance. But its particular convictions about them are drawn, not from reflection on the nature of things, but from custom and emotion. They are matters of concern rather than topics of thought. This means that in a certain sense it is indifferent to their truth. Not that popular religion lacks convictions. On the contrary, once given a conviction it can be expected to cling to it tenaciously. But it is not concerned to establish the truth by inquiry, and ground it in reasons.

What is important for popular religion is that life is beset with problems, that there is deliverance from them, that there is a path to follow, that the needed power is available, and that on these matters certitude reigns. Precisely what causes or constitutes the misery of life, what deliverance consists in, what path is to be followed, what power appealed to, what the source of this certitude: these issues are settled not on some considered principle, but by the force of feeling and tradition. In practice this allows great latitude in assigning content to convictions about them.

Salvation tends to be taken as equivalent to human well-being in the broadest sense, and whatever may contribute to it. Thus I may pray for the most immediate needs, if they have some degree of urgency. Are we in need of money? I may pray to win the lottery. Have I failed to study for an exam? I will pray to pass it. Do I need a parking spot in a hurry? As soon as any such needs become urgent enough that I feel in some sense my existence depends on them, they are gathered without difficulty under the ample umbrella of salvation.

The path to be followed embraces whatever, within the culture, looks as if it may prove effective. The repetition of a formula of words commonly held to be divine, the dropping of wooden pieces onto the ground to see how they lie, the touching of a statue, shedding the blood of a bull and letting it run over one's body, the offering of a human sacrifice: any custom hallowed by the culture may count as an efficacious means towards deliverance from ill.

In this sense popular religion is indifferent as to morals. Moral judgement properly speaking is reflective. It is also always at least potentially self-critical, while popular religion is not self-critical. If the question of morality is raised, it will take the accepted traditions of the society, and count that as morality.

In the same sense popular religion is indifferent to doctrine. Once having adopted a doctrine, it will hold onto it unquestioningly. But how the doctrine is to be justified, or what precisely it consists in, or whether it is compatible with apparently contrary beliefs, it does not enquire. In those religions that have official bodies or representatives to announce doctrine this easily leads to some tension, the officials not infrequently finding it necessary to reprove and restrain the excesses of the faithful.

For the same reason, popular religion is not particularly bothered by conceptual or practical contradictions. If I need rain for my crops while my neighbour needs dry weather, we can both hope to obtain our desired blessings, the universe being adjusted in whatever way may be necessary. Belief in a saviour and belief in one's own power to save oneself stand in some logical opposition, but popular religion typically holds to both.

In these respects, which constitute some of its characteristic features, popular religion is the same everywhere. It differs from one tradition to another only in the symbols it uses. The purpose it uses them for, the concerns it expresses in them, have everywhere the same generous latitude.

The visitor to a Buddhist temple in Japan, a Taoist temple in Taiwan, a Hindu temple in India, a mosque in Turkey or a church in Italy observes, despite great differences in appearance, an identical phenomenon. For the mass of devotees the same function is being fulfilled in each. In Hong Kong the image of divine mercy is Kuan-yin, in Lourdes Mary, but her significance to those who pray to her is the same.

Popular religion is behaviour focused on salvation in the broadest sense, without the constraints and inhibitions of deliberate reason. One result of this is that by the nature of the case it tends to give free rein to the expression of the unconscious mind. It allows the forces at work in the unconscious, the thoughts and emotions alive and effectual in the individual's life, but concealed from his conscious awareness, to manifest themselves legitimately and without shame. Thus it acts as a form of mental and emotional therapy. It also provides a fertile field of study for the psychologist.

The vehicle by which popular religion gives utterance to its concerns is the symbol, including the symbolic action of ritual. It draws its symbols from the surface structure of its culture, to turn them to its own purposes. Language it uses, not for the formulation of concepts, but as a species of ritual. Ritual is powerful for salvation in its own right, for there is no clear distinction between symbol and reality; they are one. The *ex opere operato* is a universal feature of popular religion: symbolic action has efficacy of itself, for power to wield the symbol appropriately is power over salvific reality, whatever its ultimate nature. Thus significant truth for popular religion is never the unique truth of historical events, but the timeless truth of the symbol.

An enlightening instance of the workings of popular religion in regard to issues of truth and symbolism was provided some years ago on the occasion of the Vatican's declaration that St Christopher and some other well-known saints did not exist. The protector of those who travel is called by many names. In Taiwan it is Matsu, in India, Ganesha, in Philadelphia, St Christopher. Religiously nothing could be more incongruous than to declare that this personage did not exist. It is beside the point. To those devoted to him he is real, whether a historical person of that name ever actually lived or not. The proclamation of his unreality, therefore, was taken by many, not as a well-meant attempt at a praiseworthy historical exactitude, but as an incomprehensible blow struck against the foundations of religion by its official defenders. The consternation of the faithful was provoked, not by the exposure of historical error, which it rightly considered insignificant in religion, but by the insistence of the professed guardians of religion on an irrelevant historical accuracy. They felt that something more profound was at stake than a point of history, namely an eternal truth.

Many church historians have been edified, and a few even puzzled, by the excitement and hot blood aroused in the Christian population of the fourth century by the doctrinal disputes over the Virgin Mary, taking it as evidence of a remarkable theological sophistication among the populace, now regrettably vanished. The truth is more likely that the technical theological issue was neither here nor there, but what was at stake was something simple and profound, the goddess of mercy, the Great Mother. If we view that occasion as a philosophical or theological debate, its high public passions are inexplicable. If it is seen as a manifestation of popular religion they are fairly readily comprehensible.

A person's religion is reflective to the extent that he questions his own religious assumptions, and entertains alternatives. The outcome of such questioning is twofold: justification, and criticism. It is not possible to doubt all one's assumptions at the same time. Inevitably the questioner will decide that at least some of his assumptions are justifiable. Conceivably he might decide that all of them are, but that is unlikely: more probably he will see that some are to be rejected. Thus the result of his questioning is to reinforce some convictions, and to undermine others.

The significant thing is that this occurs not haphazardly, but on some principle. A position is taken and alternatives are excluded consciously and deliberately, in virtue of some considered criterion. It is this acceptance and rejection on the basis of a criterion that makes the stance reflective, and to that extent reasonable.

The adoption of a principle excluding some possibilities and affirming others introduces a new dimension of coherence. The coherence of popular religion is the concealed and implicit coherence of the unconscious. Deliberate appeal to a principle necessitates a formal and explicit consistency. It engenders a greater measure of harmony in consciousness. The demands of conscious thought claim precedence over the needs of the unconscious.

One result of this is that symbols tend to give way to concepts as the most appropriate vehicle for expressing religious reality. The ambiguity of the symbol becomes unsatisfying. Conceptual clarity is sought. Symbols may continue to be used, but they are no longer experienced immediately as truth, they are signs standing for a reality distinct from them. Truth is no longer the truth of the symbol, but the truth of the proposition, so far as at all possible. Propositional truth is the criterion for behaviour. Myth yields to history and to philosophy.

Thus the more reflective religion becomes, the more we can expect to find a clearer and more consistent conceptual formulation of its convictions, and a logical harmony and connectedness between them.

The nature of cosmic deliverance is then specified as consisting in this rather than that, in nirvana rather than paradise, for example, or in the attainment of Brahman-atman rather than in personal immortality. The path to this deliverance is similarly specified: faith in Jesus, or observance of the Law, the Eight-fold Path, or karma yoga; in another sense, the sacrifice of Jesus or the compassion of the Buddha. The particular form ascribed to deliverance corresponds to a definite conception of human need: sin, or suffering, or finitude. The hidden power or reality by which the ultimate goal may be attained is Yahweh or the Trinity rather than Allah, or the Atman rather than the Tao. And knowledge of this is given by the Word of God, or by mystical experience, or by wisdom and insight. In each case a judgement is made in favour of one alternative rather than others, in such a way that a special, reasonably coherent interpretation of life is arrived at. Reflective religion issues in a world-view.

In the previous chapter it was noted that the world-views of religions fall into families that coincide with their cultures, especially their cultures of origin. If popular religion draws its symbols from the culture, that is, from the culture's surface structure, the world-views of reflective religion are conceptual embodiments of the interest patterns that make up the culture's hidden depth structure.

The particular forms of popular religion, for example its symbols, vary, but its function is everywhere the same. Similarly the particular forms of reflective religion, such as its world-views, vary, but its function is everywhere the same. In so far as function is important, rather than symbolic or conceptual content, devotees of popular religion have more in common with others of different traditions than they have with the more reflective forms of their own tradition; and similarly people reflective about their religion have more in common with those of other traditions than with the popular forms of their own tradition.

This account of the matter leads to the interesting question, what is the bond between the reflective and popular forms of a tradition? What connection is there between the snake handlers of Tennessee and the religion of John Calvin, between ritual ablutions in the Ganges and the sublime mysticism of the Upanishads, between the Chinese kitchen god and Confucius, or the Taoist New Year divination ceremony and the Tao Te Ching? The answer must be, not much. They share a culture. In itself that is a great deal, but not religiously. The popular religion makes use of the culture's symbols to express the most general aspirations of religion. The reflective religion embodies the culture's underlying interests, in the definite conceptual forms of a particular world-view.

In practice however the division is rarely so sharp. It is not possible to be reflective all the time. So religion is never wholly reflective, and probably also rarely or never wholly unreflective. A certain fund of symbolism is shared.

In some religious traditions a special effort has been made to keep the two together. Thus Roman Catholicism has consistently used discipline to reject the more extravagant expressions of its popular forms, and to keep the reflections of its more speculative thinkers in tight reins. By contrast Protestantism began as a highly reflective form of religion, an explicit rejection of popular Catholic Pelagianism, and with little room for the popular imagination. When popular religion eventually emerged under the Protestant banner, as was inevitable, in the absence of an external authority to restrain it it went to the opposite extreme. In general, however, the gap between the popular and reflective versions is much greater in the religions of Chinese and Indian than in those of Semitic origin. It may be speculated that this is mainly due to the legal emphasis of the Semitic religions.

To the degree that a person is given to habits of reflection in religion, he tends to feel uneasy in the presence of popular religion. If he takes part in its rituals, it is only because he can put a favourable interpretation on them, and even then he may well have reservations. The emotion it exhibits towards its symbols gives him discomfort. Its creedal formulations need adjustments to accommodate his questions, he has difficulty joining wholeheartedly in its prayers, the rhetoric of its sermons repels him.

Questioning one's own assumptions is something an individual does for himself. Thus reflection in religion is an act of withdrawal. It intensifies the inner life of the individual, making him more distinctly an individual, and more uniquely a person. By the same token it isolates him.

The defects of popular religion are not trivial. Its indifference in principle to propositional truth can lead it to extremes of gullibility. Its indifference in principle to morals renders it liable to influence by any fanaticism. It can put the greatest of energy into the worst of causes. Its merit is that it sustains devotion to the ideal simply as such and in general. But just because of this, whatever its defects, it is the fountain from which all reflective religion springs. Whenever reflective religion cuts itself off from the popular, it dries up the source of its own vitality. Reflection does not come first, but presupposes life and action. The less reflective is the root of the more reflective, and supplies it, not indeed with clarity or justification, but with nourishment and energy.

# 5 Convergence

1. Each of the major religions emerged as part of a now ancient culture. The cultures in question developed along different paths, in relative isolation, until very recently. Even now for most members of the human race cultural isolation is the ordinary condition of life.

In recent times, however, this isolation has become less impregnable in some respects. The scientific world has a global unity of standards and exchange. A network of economic interdependence embraces all the peoples of the earth. The world may not be very united, but it is more interconnected than it has ever been. A Martian visiting us 20,000 years ago would have considered the entire human race essentially a single culture. He would have more visible evidence for the view now.

If it was ever justifiable to ignore the aspects of human experience explored by cultures other than our own, it can be no longer. Each of the major cultures has made a distinctive contribution to the unfolding of the latent possibilities of human nature, and exhibits to us a different mode of being human. To the extent that they agree, they confirm the common bond of our humanity. To the extent they differ, they challenge each other: they relativise one another, implicitly criticise each other, and offer novel perspectives to be mutually absorbed and digested. The values of the traditional cultures have become the inheritance of all humanity. The same is true of their religions.

What is reasonable depends on the best evidence available. This applies also to kinds or types of religions. A species of religion that was reasonable and justified 2000 years ago may no longer be justifiable today. I believe this is true in the case of all the major religions now in existence, in their traditional forms. By reason of the cultural development just noted, the best evidence for the assessment of existing religions has been dramatically enlarged in scope. Each major world view has encountered other world views that are radically different, and that at least *prima facie* must have as solid a claim to be taken seriously. In the light of this, certain species of reflective religion especially are no longer reasonably tenable.

This charge of obsolescence can be brought against three classes of religions in particular: the so-called historical; the ethnic or national; and those that rest on an assertion of radical discontinuity, in a sense to be explained. In asserting that a class of religions is obsolete I am not maintaining that any particular religion is obsolete in its entirety, or should be abandoned wholly, since I will wish to argue later that at least certain aspects of each are of great merit and ought to be retained. What I am maintaining is that a specific principle, of fundamental import, embodied in that class of religions should be abandoned.

One of these is what may be called the principle of the historical basis. This is the conception that the foundation on which a religion rests is the divine character of a particular historical event. The religions that claim to rest on such a foundation are especially of Semitic origin:

94

Judaism, Christianity and Islam. Judaism appeals to a series of events from the migration of Abraham out of Ur to the settlement of the Hebrew tribes in Palestine; Christianity appeals to the life, death and resurrection of Jesus of Nazareth; and Islam to the inspiration that led Muhammad to write the Koran.

There are two main difficulties to basing a religion on a historical event: it is not conceptually justifiable, and it does not actually happen.

There cannot be adequate grounds for ascribing a specially divine origin to one event rather than another. For any such grounds must be either objective to some degree, or else purely private and subjective. If they are objective, i.e. a discernible feature of the historical event itself, they will be open to the public scrutiny of historical investigation and assessment, and it must be possible to reach agreement on them by using the methods of historical research, at least such agreement as historians can ever reach. But there has never been any question of this.

If the grounds are subjective, i.e. consist in a profound impression the event has made on an individual or group, then there will be as many events of divine origin among mankind as make profound impressions, and presumably if the event should cease to make a profound impression, it must cease having been of divine origin.

But in point of fact no religion ever rests on a particular historical event. The ascription of a special significance to a past event is always an act of interpretation. The basis for such an interpretation can only lie in the present, in our personal experience. It is our interpretation of our own experience of life that provides the foundation for our interpretation of history. We can understand the past only out of the present in which we stand.[1]

For example, to take the experience of Moses with the burning bush as an instance of divine revelation is to make a special presupposition, a metaphysical assumption, namely that there exists a personal God. This assumption may be true or false, but it cannot be verified by historical research. It can only be arrived at as a conclusion suggested by our own present experience of life and the world. The conceptual and logical basis of any religion is always our interpretation of our personal experience. Of course it may well be that our interpretation of our experience of life and the world is heavily coloured by the traditions we inherit. That does not alter the essential dependence of the past on the present, of our reading of history on our reading of our own lives. History cannot be explained in terms of history. The basis of a religion cannot be history, but must be that which gives the history its significance, namely, our general assumptions about the nature of the world.

If further evidence were needed to support the assertion that in point of fact religions do not rest on historical events, it can readily be found in the reactions of their adherents to evidence that the historical facts were other than they had thought. They are prepared to make the largest adjustments. Judaism has shown itself quite capable of absorbing the view that Moses did not actually exist. Christianity survived the indefinite postponement of Jesus's imminently expected return, can reconcile itself to the view that many of his apparent miracles admit of a natural explanation, and has recently demonstrated an ability, at least among some of its members, to adapt if necessary to the conclusion that he also did not exist. If a copy of the Koran were discovered that antedated

Muhammad by a hundred years, are we to expect that several million Muslims will suddenly abandon Islam? The adherents of the Semitic religions apparently realise instinctively what their theologies often do not, that their faith rests not on history, but on its coherence with their life.

A second principle that must be judged no longer tenable in religions is that of ethnic exclusiveness, i.e. the claim that membership in a particular tribe, people, nation or other civil society is a condition of participation in the religion. Surviving embodiments of this principle are the ethnic religions, such as the more traditional forms of Judaism, Shinto, a certain kind of orthodox (*Smarta*) Hinduism, and numerous local religions in primitive societies. An ethnic religion in this sense is not just any religion distinctive of a particular people. We saw in Chapter 2 that wherever there are differences in culture it is reasonable to expect there will be differences in religion. But it is quite another thing to believe that membership in a civil society automatically confers spiritual privilege.

The main arguments in defence of ethnic religions appeal to the particular and individual quality of existence. All existence is of particulars; universals are abstractions. Whatever exists is an individual, and its value is always the particular value of this individual. This applies especially to human beings, and by analogy to peoples. Every human being is unique and irreplaceable, and his value consists in his unique existence. Similarly, a people is a particular and distinct reality, and its value as an entity is always the particular value of being just this particular people. It expresses its particular character in its customs and laws, and by equal right in its

97

religion. It is entitled to follow its own path, including its own path to salvation.

Similarly, religion as such and in general does not exist: any actual religion is always a particular religion. By the nature of the case no one particular religion can be suitable for all particular people or peoples. That would be to attribute to the particular a universality it does not possess. Even if it were possible for everyone to have the same religion, it is not desirable. The right path depends on one's historical situation.

This is a powerful argument, and can scarcely fail to strike a deep chord. It appeals to one of our most profound convictions, our worth as individuals. Nevertheless the question must be asked whether it establishes what it is intended to establish. What needs to be justified is not particularity, but exclusiveness and privilege.

An ethnic religion, in the sense under discussion here, claims that there is a valid and effectual spiritual path, but that the path is reserved *a priori* to a privileged group, whose privilege stems not from any spiritual qualification, but from an accident of birth. One concomitant of this is that the religion addresses itself exclusively to them. To the rest of mankind an ethnic religion has nothing to say. Not only does it have nothing to say to them, it also has typically nothing to say about them, beyond conceding that some path to salvation is available to them. Otherwise it does not concern itself with their fate.

A first response to the argument on behalf of the ethnic religions must be that truth is universal. If a belief is true, it cannot be true only for some people and not for others. No doubt it is true that whatever exists is individual; but that itself is a universal truth. Certainly the right path depends on one's situation; but that also is a universal truth. If it is true that the Shinto Kami exist, or that the Jewish Yahweh exists, then it is true, period. It is not true at one time and false at another, or true in one place and false in another, or true for one people and not for another. If it is true that God spoke to Moses on Mt Sinai, it will always and everywhere be true that God spoke to Moses on Mt Sinai. It may be that many do not know the truth, but that does not stop it from being the truth.

If the God of Abraham, Isaac and Jacob existed, that would have drastic consequences for everyone. All of mankind, not only the Jews, must worship the God who spoke to Moses. No doubt the commandments given there were given only to the Jewish people. Does that mean that Judaism as a religion should take no account of the rest of mankind who worship, or ought to worship, its God? How can it be that the people God has spoken to have nothing to say to the people he did not speak to? Surely their very fidelity to their God would demand that they above all others concern themselves with the fate of their fellow men, since their God alone is the true God, and everyone who does not recognise him lives in spiritual darkness.

A similar argument holds in the case of Shinto. If it is the Kami who are the real sacred forces at work in the world, it is incumbent on everyone, not only the Japanese, to acknowledge them. How can the Japanese, who recognise them, have nothing to say about them to the rest of mankind who do not yet recognise them? Their very devotion to the Kami must require them to take account of the plight of their fellow men.

This argument must be judged conclusive, so far as it goes. However, it does not go as far as one might think, if put solely in terms of the truth of beliefs. It is a general feature of ethnic religions that they tend to assign a subordinate role to the truth of beliefs, or truth as propositional. They are little inclined to emphasise special doctrines. They are defined not so much by dogmas as by practices, by definite ways of living, and distinct laws and customs.

The main case against the principle of ethnic exclusiveness in religion rests not so much on a failure of logic, though there is that, as on a moral inadequacy. The ethnic isolation that may once have justified an exclusive preoccupation with the salvation of one's own people, at a time when each people could be counted on to have its own distinctive path, has now effectively dissolved. With every advance in contact between cultures the common humanity of mankind, if it was ever concealed, has emerged more clearly and unmistakably. No tongue is so alien it cannot be translated, no mentality so foreign that its kinship is not evident, no emotion so strange that it cannot be shared. For good or ill, it is the whole human race that is our family, our people. Civilisation progresses to the extent this is perceived, and the bonds linking human beings are seen to be more significant than the forces dividing them. The figure of the bodhisattva, who out of compassion for all living things vows not to enter nirvana until all can enter with him, is nobler, and obviously nobler, than that of the priest or prophet, however otherwise impressive, whose concern for humanity does not reach beyond the borders of his own people. Thus thoughtful and sensitive members of ethnic religions are in the anomalous·position of having higher standards for their own conduct than they have for their religions.

Of course, the universality of truth cannot serve to justify a religious imperialism. No doubt if a belief is true, it ought to be accepted by everyone. But it does not follow from this that there is one and only one path which all men at all times and in all circumstances ought to follow. The kind of universality we are justified in requiring of a religion is not that it insist that it and it alone is the one right religion for everybody, but that in principle and by its nature it be open and available to all men, as one effectual and legitimate path to salvation, accessible to any when and if the time and circumstances of their life commend it, not the restricted possession of a group specially set apart by birth, and equally not claiming to be the only valid path.

(It should be evident that these observations do not touch the right of a people to exist. There is a clear conceptual and logical distinction between a people and their religion, and they are physically separable, in that the non-existence of the religion does not entail the non-existence of the people. The Japanese are capable of surviving without Shinto; the Jewish people can get along without the Jewish religion, and have already demonstrated their ability to do so in Israel. If all Jews were Buddhists, the Jewish people could still exist; if the Japanese became Muslim, it would not mean their end as a people.)

The third principle to be objurgated in religion is of a somewhat different nature from the other two. It distinguishes not so much a class of traditions as a way of being religious. It is the conception that the realm of salvation is totally discontinuous from the present life. In this kind of religion the realm of salvation is so far removed from the world of ordinary experience that no categories of thought apply to it, no language can meaningfully be used of it, and the canons of reason are confounded in its ultimate paradox.

This species of religiousness is moved by a laudable desire to exalt the ideal and the transcendent to its due altitude above the mundane. But the consequences of this removal are portentous. The present life is first simply negated, and attention is devoted entirely to the Wholly Other, where lies salvation. But there is no bridge from here to there. The farther shore has been transported to such a distance it has become simply remote. The Other proves to be nothingness. Religious fervour must then fall back into what alone is accessible, the mundane. The logical consequence is a purely secular gospel.

A disastrous feature of this kind of religion, where it is consistent, is the denial of reason. Reason becomes the enemy of salvation. It is not merely assigned a provisional role, to be left behind once deliverance is attained, but declared a foe, an arch-obstruction, a chain shackling the spirit, not an instrument of our salvation, but part of our predicament. I have in mind, in varying degrees, such figures as Nagarjuna and Shankara, the Ch'an masters and Suzuki, Luther, Kierkegaard, and Karl Barth.

It is not hard to show that this kind of religion is mistaken. There can only possibly be one world. For if we postulate two worlds, they could only be two in virtue of some difference, and a difference already implies a relationship, a connection, and presupposes other connections, so that they make up, after all, one world. There cannot possibly be a *wholly* Other.

Similarly there is little difficulty in demonstrating that hostility to reason is unreasonable, or that rejection of justification can scarcely be justifiable. But the effort is wasted. This kind of religion has declared itself in advance immune to argument. Let it be refuted a thousand times over, it scorns refutation. It may be proven not only false but absurd: it delights in the absurdity.

On the other hand, if the arguments against it are without force in its eyes, so must any arguments on its behalf be. If its refutation will not convert adherents, neither can its justification. There can be no reason why anyone should accept it.

Where reason's arguments are rendered futile in principle, all that remains is an appeal to the intuition of values. It is true that the power of reason has sometimes been exaggerated. But a delight in unreason is retrograde and decadent. Reason alone may not be able to save us, but that does not mean it is our enemy. If it is not our salvation, it does not on that account become our damnation. The fact that an ideal is not lived up to does not discredit the ideal, and abuses of reason do nothing to discredit reason. The belief that salvation is to be found in the annihilation of reason can only be fatal. One rapid and typical consequence is the betrayal of history as a field of significant endeavour. Thus Zen abandons not only its own history, but any involvement in history, a feature that has rendered it helpless to respond to the spiritual challenge of Marxism.

2. If it is true that all major existing religions must be judged obsolete, for the reason that they are the work of cultural isolations now passed, it is also true that each speaks on behalf of a large area of human experience, and the question must be asked whether each does not inevitably have its own distinctive contribution to make

to the spiritual future of a more interrelated mankind. This is especially true of the three great families of the major religions, the Indian, the Chinese, and the Semitic. If the breadth and depth of human experience is to be of account, no religion will be adequate which ignores the separate messages coming from such vast constituencies.

In each of these religious cultures at least one principle may be discerned which is central to it and distinctive of it, and which any religious philosophy that desires to be even minimally adequate to the range of human experience must embody. Each represents a different perspective on life, and entails a different way of living. These principles will be simply stated here without an attempt, which would go beyond the scope of this essay, to bring them into a coherent synthesis. But it may be observed that as far as we can tell we have no grounds for giving greater weight to one than to the others.

The three principles are:

that man surpasses nature
that man is part of nature
that the individual self is to be transcended.

The statement that man surpasses nature points to the chasm that separates those beings that are persons from those that are not. Personhood is the realm of mind, of moral worth and spiritual striving. A person is a unique being, with a unique dignity, and is not replaceable by another. This is true only of persons. They are the foremost entities in the world, and we can conceive of no category of being that would be higher. As a result, human beings necessarily have certain claims, at the least by way of appropriateness, on one another. A person's

quality as a person depends on how he responds to these
claims. Thus being a person is always in a special sense a
being-with other persons. The factor of most significance
in the life of any person is his relationship with other
persons. Of all entities, only human beings can fall away
from their own nature. A seagull can never be ungull-
like, or a dog anything but doggy. But a human being can
be inhuman, because he can fail to treat his fellow human
beings appropriately. By the same token, being a bird or
a dog is simply a fact. But being human is not only a fact
but also an ideal, to be striven for, and perhaps never to
be attained. Thus an unbridgeable gulf separates persons
from all other things. They are not reducible to non-
personal factors.

The unique dignity of human beings shows itself with
special force in its confident assurance that in some
respects it stands outside the dominion of time and space.
It can possess Truth, which is eternal. It can assert
Goodness, as an absolute. It has typically refused to
accept the notion that it simply perishes. Other creatures
may well come and go, but it is intolerable that persons
should cease, should be merely transient. Once we exist,
we should continue to exist. As a final end death has not
been generally acceptable to men, though bitter fact may
compel them to come to terms with it.

The preceding statements purport only to describe
certain states of affairs. When used for that purpose they
may well occur in the context of a non-religious philosophy. But religious thought is not interested in the
description of facts for their own sake. It is intent on
deliverance, and the path to it, and the predicament that
requires it. When a religious world-view states that man
surpasses nature, it is not intending primarily to describe

a fact for the sake of the fact, but for practical reasons, to point to a particular predicament we find ourselves in, the nature of deliverance from it, and the path that will lead to that deliverance.

Our predicament as human beings in this perspective is that we are deficient in humanity, or, what is the same thing, that we fail to treat our fellow human beings fittingly. The only salvation open to us must lie in the opposite of this, the achievement of true and full humanity. The path to that goal consists in striving to treat our fellow human beings ever more appropriately. Our dealings with the non-personal world of things, the world we call nature, must be wholly subservient to the striving for humanity.

This general perspective on life has been expressed powerfully in the injunctions to love one's enemy, and to act towards others as we wish them to act towards us.

In the present era this perspective has acquired a new dimension through the recognition of the special power of social structures. Social structures have the ability to take on a certain independent existence, as it were a life of their own, governing by their own intrinsic power the interactions of the human beings who create and sustain them. This recognition has issued in the movement for social justice, which must be regarded as the most significant event of the modern age. Not merely the characters of individuals, as in the past, but the legal, economic and even linguistic structures of society must be transformed to confer equality on disadvantaged minorities and the underprivileged of every sort. The movement is part of the general trend of history towards the equality of all human beings. Its scope is global, differing as between communist, capitalist and developing societies only in emphasis. It is not only irresistible in the long run, but, despite profound inadequacies, such as its current dominance by a conflict model of social evolution, manifestly right in its central intention. Any religion from now on, to be adequate to our experience of life, must assign to the quest for social justice not merely a marginal but an essential place. As yet, however, this is not true of any existing religion.

The contrasting statement that man is *part* of nature points to the *continuity* between persons and all other beings. It does not mean that part of man is part of nature, as if there were only some portion or aspect of human reality that belonged within the realm of nature, and another that did not. It means that human reality in its entirety falls within the domain we call nature. Human nature is continuous with all the other natures of things.

Perhaps the most striking form this continuity takes is the emergence of persons from non-personal entities. The best evidence substantiates the view that human beings are a product of the evolution of non-human beings. Substances that were not persons have changed into persons, non-human beings have become human. What was once seaweed is now a man. This evolutionary drama would only be possible if there were an essential continuity of nature between them.

But apart from any theory of evolution there is the consideration that a thing can exist only if its nature fits in with the natures of other things. Elephants continue to exist, dodos do not, and banshees, so far as we know, never have, because the universe is hospitable to elephants, but ceased to be to dodos, and never was to banshees. There is a harmony between the natures of all existing things, as a condition of their existence.

At bottom the same forces are at work in mind as in matter, in thought and feeling as in the growth of trees and the dying of stars; the same fundamental laws govern intellect and will as electrons or the family cat. This truth was grasped profoundly by Dylan Thomas:

The force that through the green fuse drives the flower
Drives my green age; that blasts the roots of trees
Is my destroyer.
And I am dumb to tell the crooked rose
My youth is bent by the same wintry fever.

Persons cannot 'master', in the sense of dominate, nature and its laws. They can discover them, and take better account of them, but how could persons be their masters when it is they that give persons their powers? Anything mind achieves, it achieves by respecting the natures of things and obeying the laws of nature, not by commanding them.

Furthermore, nature exhibits a painful impartiality in the treatment it accords its citizens. The universe does not single persons out for special favour. So far as we can tell, it sets no greater store by them than by any other thing, is neither more friendly to them nor more hostile. It has so far encouraged their existence; sometimes it bestows well-being on them and sometimes ill—when not by the operation of inexorable laws, then by accident— and in the end it brings all to a like fate.

Thus we have no reason to divorce nature and culture, or nature and art. Culture is part of nature. It is in and through culture that we discover what is truly natural. And culture is that area where nature itself can become unnatural. Similarly, history must be seen as part of nature, and not as something to be set over against nature or in contrast to it.

In the previous section the term nature referred, by definition, to that which is not personal. Here, however, it cannot mean that, since persons are here declared to be part of nature. Nor can it mean simply the universe, or the sum total of what is, because in that sense it is obvious that man is part of nature, but the statement intends to say something that, at least in the West, has been far from obvious. I take the notion of nature here to refer in general to the realm of elements, structures, or functions that persons and the non-personal have in common, apart from the fact of existence. These elements are qualities of various sorts, and it is the inherent qualities of things that make up their natures. Thus persons themselves have a nature, a particular way of being as persons; and if they are to exist, their nature must be compatible with the natures of other existing things. Nature is the sum total of *talia*, or suchness.

Perhaps one reason why it has not been generally obvious in the West that persons are part of nature may have been the problem of freedom, both external or legal, and inner freedom of the will, which has been a special preoccupation of the West. Can we say that a free action of a person has its origin in his nature? If we say yes, that seems tantamount to admitting that what we call a free action is in fact determined. But if we concede that human actions are determined, the purpose of law, both social and moral, historically so important to the West, becomes unclear.

The view defended here points to a different aspect of the problem. It is precisely what we understand by the nature of a person, to have freedom of will, that is, to be able either to will or not to will, and to choose between alternatives. On the other hand, the range of his choices and actions is both made possible and at the same time circumscribed in advance by his nature. Whatever he does, it must be natural for him to do it, not in the justifying sense that his nature is fulfilled by it, but in the descriptive sense that his nature permits it. It will not on that account be necessary. In this sense, there can be nothing that is not natural. It is of the nature of a free action, however, that it does not necessarily improve the quality of the person doing it. In this sense, which is evaluative, it may be against his nature.

Again, these statements about the place of persons in nature may be taken as merely describing certain facts, and to this end may well figure in a non-religious philosophy. But in the context of a religious world-view the assertion that man is part of nature is not a statement about detached, objective reality for its own sake, but an utterance about the predicament we find ourselves in as human beings, the nature of deliverance from it, and the path that will lead to that deliverance.

Our predicament, in this perspective, is that we are that sole realm where nature can turn against itself and fall out of harmony with itself. We can lose touch, in our very being, with the fittingness that pervades the world. This is the source of failure and frustration. Successful living or salvation lies in regaining the original harmony of being, the appropriateness inherent in nature. The path to that goal lies in respecting and fitting in with the natures of things, not obtruding ourselves, not expecting extraordinary favours from the cosmos because we are persons, not absolutising our human perspectives on things or the special values of humanity, but accepting with an even mind the inherent limitations of our being, because they are themselves constitutive for our being.

The third statement, that the individual self is to be transcended, points to an ideal, which has what may be considered a negative and an affirmative aspect. The one is total detachment from the individual self. This has been recommended on purely pragmatic grounds, that we suffer because we are attached to ourselves, and if we cease to be attached to ourselves we will cease to suffer. But that is liable to appear a curiously selfish ground for selflessness. There are better reasons for commending a total detachment from oneself. Rightly understood, it seems to be of the essence of the highest spirituality. Mankind in general recognises intuitively that unselfishness is always a noble achievement, and total unselfishness a lofty ideal.

It is sometimes felt, however, that an ideal of total detachment from oneself, and from the particularity of one's own concerns, militates against that healthy regard for ourselves which common sense suggests. Jesus enjoined us to love our neighbour as ourselves, which implies that we ought to love ourselves; the Buddhist tradition encourages the practice of friendliness towards oneself; and sound psychology tells us that often the reason why we detest others is that unconsciously we cannot stand ourselves. If we become totally detached from ourselves, what will happen with the necessary defense of our rights, for example?

But there is no incompatibility between a due esteem of oneself and total detachment from oneself. On the contrary, detachment from oneself is a condition of a proper love for oneself. The virtue of friendliness towards oneself is not egotism, or narcissism. It is a species-friendliness. It means that I have the same regard or compassion for myself that I have for others. I have it towards myself as a member of a species, because I am this kind of being, and so I have an equal love for all members of my kind. Species-love in this sense should not be understood as necessarily entailing a commitment to the biological continuance of the species itself. It is conceivable that in order to be true to its own nature the species must be prepared to undergo extinction, for example in defense of a moral principle. Love for the human species is a love for actually existing persons, not for merely possible ones.

It requires a detachment from the particularity and individuality of myself, which makes possible a universal love that also includes myself. By contrast, egotism and narcissism are a love for myself solely as this particular individual, and not at all as a member of a species, sharing the same nature and dignity with others. A defence of my rights is spiritually legitimate when it is equally a defence of the rights of others. A defence of my rights exclusively as rights of this particular individual, though it may not be morally wrong, is spiritually retrograde. Also, the notion is probably logically incoherent, in that it is the possession of human nature which enables us to be the subject of rights.

The conviction of the intrinsic goodness of selflessness as a virtue has sometimes been so strong as to lead to a denial of the actual existence of the individual self, or the assignment to it of only a relative reality. In this case selflessness becomes a descriptive term for the actual being of persons, independently of their virtue.

As a positive ideal self-transcendence has been conceived of variously. According to one conception it consists in the realisation of one's identity with absolute reality, or with Emptiness. But this makes metaphysical assumptions, the truth of which is by no means obvious. According to another view, it consists in a wholehearted devotion to the welfare of other persons, or of all sentient beings.

Two statements in particular have formulated this latter ideal sublimely. One is the injunction of Jesus to love one's neighbour as oneself, and to love one's enemy. The other, perhaps even more impressive, as an expression of the ideal of boundless compassion, because it sees that ideal exemplified in the highest reality itself, is the marvellous utterance of Shinran: If even the good will be saved, how much more the wicked! No loftier ideal has been proposed to mankind than this, I believe, and conceivably none can be.

# Retrospect

What has been gained by these reflections? Five main theses have been propounded.

1. The common theme of religion is cosmic deliverance. Religion can be defined as behaviour focused on cosmic deliverance, and 'a religion' is a way of life similarly focused. This is against the widely defended view that the variety of religious phenomena makes it neither possible nor desirable to attribute a common denominator or 'essence' to them, and that we must therefore be content to discover family resemblances among them. The definition provides a criterion for deciding in what sense, if any, such things as ethics or psychology can count as religion, as some wish to claim.

2. Their focus on cosmic deliverance means that all religions are elaborations of a basic psychological dynamic, which is also a logical structure, containing three elements: cosmic complaint, cosmic deliverance, and passage from the one to the other. Particular religions are cultural embodiments of this dynamic. All the features that diversify and distinguish one religion from another, including their truth-claims, are culturally determined. It follows from this that in any encounter or conflict between religions or religious truth-claims, what is really at issue is the priority of their cultural values, so that there

is a certain naivety in attempting to settle questions of religious truth on their own terms, without reference to their cultural substructure.

3. The particularities of religions, the terms of their cosmic complaint and their images of deliverance, owe their actual existence, without exception, to historical accident. The geography of the spirit is profoundly fortuitous.

4. Religion is never rational, if by rational is meant originating from the activity of reasoning. Religion is always rational, if by rational is meant susceptible of explanation. If by rational we mean infused by reflection, some forms of religion are significantly less rational than others. To the extent that a particular manifestation of religion lacks reflection it is indifferent to truth and to morals, being preoccupied with the quest for deliverance. It lives out of the unconscious, and its logic is the logic of the unconscious. To the extent that religion is governed by reflection it acquires the great virtue of reasonableness, and a corresponding esteem for truth and morals; but it then easily loses its vitality, becoming more remote from its roots, which are prereflective.

5. The major religions emerged in cultures relatively isolated and now ancient. They are each in some vital respect obsolete, yet each also speaks on behalf of a large constituency of human experience. To do justice to the past, religious reflection must attempt a synthesis of its now global heritage. To do justice to the present, it must do so critically and self-critically, accepting nothing merely on the grounds of personal loyalty to a particular tradition.

# Prospect

If the analysis of religion given here is correct, especially that in the first chapter, then the future of religion, and particularly of any reasonable religion, must be intimately linked with the question: Is there after all, a cosmic deliverance? Is there really any salvation? What is the best that we have realistic grounds to hope for? This question leads beyond the bounds of the present essay; however in the judgement of the author it is without doubt the most pressing question in religion, and for the answer we must now look, not so much to religion, but to the philosophy of religion—if indeed it can be answered at all.

# Notes

INTRODUCTION

1. I am indebted to Professor Marvin Shaw, of the University of Montana, for several of the formulations in this paragraph.

CHAPTER I

1. Zen Buddhism maintains a degree of life in some academic and philosophical circles in Japan. Otherwise Buddhism in Asia is purely devotional. In the face of the challenge of communism it has shown itself ideologically impotent, and having lost mainland China is now only a remnant of what it was. Whatever intellectual vitality Taoism has is derived from the efforts of the laymen of the National Taoist Association in Taiwan, but the professional priesthood of the Northern party lacks the rudiments of education.

In India devotional religion flourishes, but the ancient great tradition of religious thought appears almost extinct. Religious India continues on as if the intellectual forces of the modern world did not exist.

In the Islamic world the picture is similar: fierce attachment to tradition, with a few enlightened men trying to come to grips with the intellectual difficulties of modernity.

Although Jews have long been among the intellectual leaders of the West, their best energies seem to have gone into fields other than religion: the leaders of Judaism have only recently begun to take account of the problems raised for their religion by critical thinking.

Of all the major religions only Christianity has really faced up to the problems of contemporary critical thought: and it has been intellectually paralysed as a result. Many Christians are currently

119

engaged in a struggle to overcome this paralysis, but so far the outcome must be considered still in doubt.

2. Cf. Melville Herskovits, 'A culture is the way of life of a people', *Cultural Anthropology* (New York: Knopf, 1955).
3. C. Kluckhohn and W. H. Kelly, 'The concept of culture', in R. Linton (ed.), *The Science of Man in the World Crisis* (New York: Columbia University Press, 1945).
4. *A Common Faith* (New Haven: Yale University Press, 1960) p.8.
5. Thus W. Cantwell Smith in *The Meaning and End of Religion* (New York: Mentor Books, 1964) Ch. 3.
6. *A Common Faith*, Ch. 1.

CHAPTER 2

1. Heinrich Zimmer has argued these cultural differences in Joseph Campbell (ed.), *Philosophies of India* (New York: Pantheon Books, 1951).
2. The cultural distinction has been argued by, for example, Hu Shih 'Religion and philosophy in Chinese history', in Sophia H. Chen Zen (ed.), *Symposium on Chinese Culture* (New York: Paragon Book Reprint Corp., 1969); Yong Yap and Arthur Cotterell, *The Early Civilization of China* (London: Weidenfeld & Nicolson, 1975).

CHAPTER 3

1. L. W. King and R. C. Thompson, *Inscriptions of Darius the Great* (London, 1907); F. H. Weissbach and W. Bang, *Die altpersischen Keilinschriften* (Leipzig: J. C. Hinrichs, 1908). The Gathas of Zoroaster and other inscriptions of the Persian emperors present vivid illustrations of the same order. Darius equates rebellion against himself with rebellion against God: 'O man, do not let the command of God seem repugnant to you. Do not leave the right path: do not rise in rebellion.'
2. Friedrich Heer, *The Intellectual History of Europe*, Vol. 1, tr. J. Steinberg (New York: Doubleday, 1966).
3. Ibid.
4. Franz Cumont, *Lux Perpetua* (Paris: P. Geuthner, 1949).

5. As any biblical scholar will recognise, this account is greatly oversimplified; in particular it passes over the early development of the Christian movement in Palestine. But it is only the broad outlines of the story that I wish to tell.

CHAPTER 4

1. Michel Foucault, *The Order of Things* (London: Tavistock Press, 1970) Ch. 2.

CHAPTER 5

1. A similar argument has been advanced by A. N. Whitehead, *Religion in the Making* (Cambridge University Press, 1926) Ch. III, p. 1, but seems to have had little impact.

# Index